AF608086

THE CATHOLIC UNIVERSITY OF AMERICA
CANON LAW STUDIES
No. 127

The Extrajudicial Coercive Powers Of Ecclesiastical Superiors

AN HISTORICAL SYNOPSIS AND COMMENTARY

A DISSERTATION

Submitted to the Faculty of Canon Law of the Catholic University of America in Partial Fulfillment of the Requirements for the Degree of Doctor of Canon Law

BY

ANTHONY ALBERT ESSWEIN, J.C.L.
Priest of the Archdiocese of St. Louis

THE CATHOLIC UNIVERSITY OF AMERICA PRESS
WASHINGTON, D. C.
1941

NIHIL OBSTAT:

JEROME D. HANNAN, S.T.D., J.C.D.

Censor Deputatus.

IMPRIMATUR:

✠JOHN J. GLENNON, S.T.D.

Archiepiscopus Sancti Ludovici.

St. Louis, May 5, 1941

MURRAY & HEISTER
WASHINGTON, D. C.

PRINTED BY

TIMES AND NEWS PUBLISHING CO.
GETTYSBURG, PA., U. S. A.

TO

MY FATHER AND MOTHER

TABLE OF CONTENTS

Foreword ix

CHAPTER ONE

Coercive Powers of the Church 1

PART ONE—HISTORICAL SYNOPSIS

CHAPTER TWO

Supreme Jurisdiction in the Church 8
The Pope 8

CHAPTER THREE

Participants in the Supreme Jurisdiction in the Church 16
Article I. The Patriarch 16
Article II. The Metropolitan 18
Article III. Vicars and Prefects Apostolic; Abbots and Prelates *Nullius* 24

CHAPTER FOUR

Episcopal Jurisdiction in the Church 25
The Bishop 25

CHAPTER FIVE

Participants in the Episcopal Jurisdiction in the Church 37
Article I. The Archdeacon 37
Article II. The Vicar General 42
Article III. The Officialis 44
Article IV. The Pastor 48

PART TWO—CANONICAL COMMENTARY

CHAPTER SIX

Ecclesiastical Superiors Possessing Coercive Powers 51
Article I. Supreme Jurisdiction in the Church 53
A. The Pope 53
Article II. Participants in the Supreme Jurisdiction in the Church 56
A. The Ecumenical Council 56
B. The Cardinals 57
C. The Sacred Congregations 58
D. The Patriarch 60
E. The Metropolitan 60
F. Plenary and Provincial Councils 61
G. Vicars and Prefects Apostolic; Abbots and Prelates *Nullius* 63
H. Apostolic Administrators 64
Article III. Episcopal Jurisdiction in the Church 65
A. The Bishop 65
Article IV. Participants in the Episcopal Jurisdiction in the Church 68
A. Vicar Capitular or Administrator 68
B. Vicar General 70
C. Officialis or Judge 71

CHAPTER SEVEN

Subject of Coercive Powers of Superiors 73
Article I. Those Having Domicile or Quasi-Domicile 73
Article II. Transients or Peregrini 79
Article III. Exempt Religious 83

CHAPTER EIGHT

Reservation of Penalties 94

CHAPTER NINE

INFLICTION OF COERCIVE MEASURES 101
Article I. Requisites of Superiors 101
Article II. Penal Remedies 102
Article III. The Precept 106
Article IV. Penalties that May be Inflicted *Per Modum Praecepti* 110

CHAPTER TEN

EXTRAORDINARY PROCEDURE OF CANON 2222 115
Article I. In Case of Grave Scandal or Serious Transgression 115
Article II. Probable or Prescribed Delicts 119
CONCLUSIONS 128
BIBLIOGRAPHY 129
ABBREVIATIONS 134
BIOGRAPHICAL NOTE 135
ALPHABETICAL INDEX 136
CANON LAW STUDIES 138

FOREWORD

It is the purpose of this dissertation to offer, in the first place, a historical study of the exercise of extrajudicial coercive power by ecclesiastical superiors, excluding religious superiors, who in the past have exercised this power in the Church; and secondly, to offer a commentary upon those canons which deal with the superiors who now possess coercive jurisdiction and the exercise of this jurisdiction in an extrajudicial manner through the use of the precept.

As the Table of Contents will show, the historical section has been divided into two general divisions: the exercise of the supreme jurisdiction and the exercise of episcopal jurisdiction in the Church. Each of these divisions is then further subdivided in accordance with whether the individual superiors participate in the supreme or only in the episcopal jurisdiction. Since, on the one hand, these offices did not arise simultaneously and, on the other hand, did not all enjoy the same permanency, it was considered better to treat the whole matter in a logical rather than a chronological order, retaining the chronological development in each office only in as far as this was possible.

The second part of the dissertation is a commentary on the law as it now is. Superiors who today possess coercive jurisdiction are considered, and the basis for such powers is established. For the exercise of jurisdiction there must necessarily be subjects; who these are, and in what things they are subject to the ecclesiastical superior, is discussed in the following chapter. In the imposition of a penalty, the superior may wish to reserve the remission of the particular penal measure to himself; if this is desired he must comply with certain rules which are analyzed at length. The procedure to be followed in the imposition of extrajudicial coercive measures will present problems of its own; such a subject naturally calls for a careful study, and to this the fourth chapter of this section is devoted. In the final chapter there are considered two exceptional procedures, the first of which empowers the superior to act immediately and without warning when great scandal or exceptional malice exists, while the second is not, strictly taken, a penal measure but one closely akin, consisting in the refusal to promote to higher orders, in the prohibition to exercise the sacred ministry and in the non-penal removal from office for prescribed or probable crimes.

The writer takes this occasion to express his gratitude to His Excellency, John J. Glennon, S.T.D., Archbishop of St. Louis, for the opportunity offered for advanced study. He is also deeply appreciative of the help, guidance and suggestions so generously offered by the members of the Faculty of the School of Canon Law. A word of thanks is also due to the Very Rev. Mark K. Carroll for his innumerable acts of kindness and solicitude. To the Very Rev. John P. Cody, Ph.D., S.T.D., J.C.D.; to the Rev. Mark S. Ebner, J.C.L.; and to the Rev. Wm. Drumm, J.C.B., and to all who helped in the preparation of this work, grateful acknowledgment is made for their suggestions and assistance.

CHAPTER I

Coercive Powers of the Church

"Nativum et proprium Ecclesiae ius est, independens a qualibet humana auctoritate, coercendi delinquentes sibi subditos poenis tum spiritualibus tum etiam temporalibus." (Can. 2214, § 1.)

Before considering the coercive rights of the Church, one may well recall the essential characteristics of every perfect society. Such a society must necessarily be complete and juridically independent; complete, that is, possessing the means required to realize the end for which it was created; independent, that is, tending to an end not subordinated to that of a society other than itself.[1] Having these characteristics, by its very nature a perfect society has certain inalienable rights. Among these is the right to legislate for its own welfare and to judge in conformity with the laws enacted. Such prerogatives, however, could not be objectively realized unless there were existent at the same time the right to use means, proportionate and apt, for the realization of the ends for which the particular society was established.[2] Men endowed by their Creator with the faculties of intellect and will are essentially rational, and as such are expected to act in accordance with the nature they possess. Not always, however, do human beings act in conformity with reason; not always do men seek the higher and perhaps more remote good in preference to the proximate; not always are they possessed of those principles that would motivate them to subject individual likes to

[1] Cavagnis, *Institutiones Iuris Publici Ecclesiastici* (2. ed., 2 vols., Rome, 1888), I, 31; Cappello, *Summa Iuris Publici Ecclesiastici* (2. ed., Romae: Apud Aedes Universitatis Gregorianae, 1928), p. 67; Ottaviani, *Institutiones Iuris Publici Ecclesiastici* (2. ed., 2 vols., Typis Polyglottis Vaticanis, 1936), I, 57.

[2] Cappello, *op. cit.*, pp. 70, 75; Cavagnis, *op. cit.*, p. 72; Ottaviani, *op. cit.*, I, nn. 43, 46.

corporate good and advantage. Under such conditions a perfect society often finds itself compelled to inflict upon recalcitrant members measures destined to produce the end intended.[3]

If these are the rights of a perfect society, the Church certainly possesses them. The canon cited above vindicates to the Church a right derived from her very constitution, the right to punish by either spiritual or temporal means, those of her subjects who act in opposition to her decrees. It is a natural right (*nativum*), and not one acquired from an external authority, for it flows from the fact that the Church is a juridic society, established by Christ as an organization of men having the same common faith, the same authority to which all are subject, the same common means, and destined for a supernatural end.[4] Christ, in establishing His Church, pointed out that as there is one Lord, so also is there "one faith and one baptism";[5] so also is there but "one fold and one shepherd."[6] In forming His Church, Christ so ordained things that there would be one supreme ruler over all, giving universal power and authority to this one to "bind and loose."[7] Her end is a supernatural one, to lead men to a supernatural and eternal destiny, than which no more excellent or more noble can exist.[8] Nor did her founder fail to give the means to achieve this high purpose, for He entrusted to her spiritual means, the sacraments, by the use of which men may be better able to arrive at the supernatural end for which they were created. The Church, therefore, possesses formally and immediately that which is required to reach the end for which it was established, and thus it is independent of human societies that have for their purpose the natural and material welfare of human beings.[9]

Christ, sending forth His apostles, commanded them to teach

---

[3] Cappello, *op. cit.*, pp. 77, 78; Ottaviani, *op. cit.*, I, n. 61.

[4] Cappello, *op. cit.*, pp. 138, 139; Cavagnis, *op. cit.*, p. 117; Ottaviani, *op. cit.*, I, n. 90.

[5] Eph. IV, 6.

[6] John X, 16; Eph. IV, 15.

[7] Math. XVI, 19.

[8] Cappello, *op. cit.*, p. 137.

[9] Cappello, *op. cit.*, p. 138.

all nations.[10] In speaking thus to His apostles, He, by emphasizing the fact that "all power is given to me in heaven and in earth,"[11] signified that He was giving to them the plenitude of the power He Himself possessed. The apostles went forth, therefore, not merely to teach the doctrine that must be believed but also the precepts that must be observed; their work was not merely to be custodians and guardians of revealed truth, but also to make known the precepts which were a necessary complement and determinant of the law as preached by the Master. Since the precepts of the Gospels remained indeterminate in part, there was necessarily postulated in the apostolic college a legislative power that would further elucidate them.[12] Finally, there was given to the Church the power to decide in particular instances the practical application of laws which she had enacted and to issue authentic declarations and decrees in accordance therewith.[13]

It is not enough, however, for the Church, in order to achieve the purpose and end of its existence, merely to enact laws and to exercise judicial power. It is necessary besides that she be able to compel compliance from those who are reluctant, to restrain the transgressors of the law, and to punish the contumacious, so that the perversely inclined may not be free to transgress her laws or spurn her decrees.[14]

The Church, then, was not destined merely to be a teaching society, one that exercises mere persuasive or moral power over her members, but one that was also to be competent to demand compliance with the truths it taught and the decrees it enacted. To it was given whatever power was required to achieve the end of its establishment—the common and individual spiritual welfare of men. No limitation whatever was placed on the power to bind and loose: a power that applied to all those who are her subjects, those brought under her jurisdiction through Bap-

---

[10] Math. XXVII, 20.

[11] Math. XXVIII, 18.

[12] Cappello, *op. cit.*, p. 191; Ottaviani, *op. cit.*, I, nn. 123, 127.

[13] Math. XVIII, 16, 17; cf. Cappello, *op. cit.*, p. 219; Ottaviani, *op. cit.*, I, n. 145.

[14] Cappello, *op. cit.*, p. 233; Cavagnis, *op. cit.*, p. 175; Ottaviani, *op. cit.*, I, n. 164.

tism.[15] In virtue of the power to bind and loose, Christ gave His Church the power to separate from her fold those of her members who refused compliance; and what is this power, but one instance of the power of using coercive measures?

The right of the Church to use coercive measures is further described in the canon as a *"ius proprium,"* "not merely in the sense of possession, but of a characteristic power."[16] She possesses this power in virtue of her origin and constitution; and not from the fact that it was delegated to her by a power or authority foreign to herself. The power which the Church exercises is not an end in itself; rather it is to be used to attain the end and purpose of her existence. Being a spiritual society, she must necessarily make use of means in conformity with her nature. Thus it is that the spiritual element must prevail, and thus it is that the coercive measures imposed by her consist chiefly of censures, having for their purpose the reformation of the guilty. As a *perfect* society, the Church directly and immediately looks to the external and spiritual welfare conformable to her nature, seeking the sanctification of all members in as much as they are a part of the external society. Being a perfect *spiritual* society, however, destined by its constitution to promote the sanctification of its individual members, it must be concerned about properly disposing its members toward their Creator, that thus they may tend to eternal life.[17]

Finally, this power is spoken of as independent of all human authority (*independens a qualibet humana auctoritate*). This characteristic of the coercive power of the Church follows as a corollary from the fact that coercive power is a *"ius nativum,"* a constitutional right. Derived from the very essence of the Church as established by Christ, it is a divine right, and has, as its source, an authority higher than any human authority. No human authority can therefore attack it with impunity.

Although the Church has always claimed this power for herself,

---

[15] Math. XVIII, 17.

[16] Augustine, *A Commentary on the New Code of Canon Law* (8 vols., St. Louis, Herder), Vol. VIII (3. ed., 1931), 59.

[17] Michiels, Gommarus, *De Delictis et Poenis* (Lublin-Polonia, 1934), I, 20.

and although the popes had exercised coercive powers in the universal Church, it was frequently found necessary to reaffirm the right of the Church in the matter. Thus Pope Boniface VIII, already in the fourteenth century pointed out in his bull *Unam Sanctam* that in the control of the Church are two powers, the spiritual and the secular; the spiritual is wielded in the Church by the priests, the secular is to be employed for the Church by the civil authority, always under the direction of the spiritual power. Since the spiritual power is the higher, it has a right to establish and guide the secular power, being itself subject to the higher power of God. Although this spiritual authority is exercised by men, it is not a human authority but divine, for the commission to exercise it was received from Christ Himself.[18]

Later, in the same century, the errors of Marsilius of Padua were propagated.[19] Marsilius completely abandoned the old theocratic conception of society and found the basis of all power in the will of the people. He claimed that all ecclesiastical power had its source in the community and in the Emperor who was the principal representative of that community. The power of the lay state was unlimited, he contended, for the Church had no sovereign, visible head, and the Pontiff had only as much power as the state granted him. Thus the pope became wholly subject to and dependent on the civil ruler; the secular power was supreme, the spiritual subservient. The universal Church, in his mind, could not inflict a coercive measure upon anyone, unless this power was given by the Emperor.[20] In his bull of October 23, 1327, Pope John XXII suspended and excommunicated Marsilius and his abettor, Jean de Jandun, whom he called "duos perditionis filios et maledictionis alumnos."[21]

---

[18] Denzinger-Bannwart, *Enchiridion Symbolorum* (16. et 17. eds., Freiburgi Brisgoviae: Herder, 1928), n. 469; Kirsch, "Unam Sanctam," *Catholic Encyclopedia,* XV, 528.

[19] Together with Jean de Jandun, a canon of Senlis, Marsilius composed the "Defensor Pacis." This work was finished as early as June 6, 1324; it was printed in 1522, and placed on the Index of Forbidden Books in 1559.—Salambier, "Marsilius of Padua," *Catholic Encyclopedia,* IX, 719.

[20] Denzinger-Bannwart, *Enchiridion Symbolorum,* nn. 497-499.

[21] Const. *"Licet,"* 23 oct. 1327—*Fontes,* n. 38.

In the Synod of Pistoia (1786) this power was similarly denied. Among the decrees of the Synod is found the statement that the Church did not have given her by Christ any coercive power which enabled her to enforce her laws and precepts; the only power given her was that of counsel and persuasion. This error was condemned as heretical by Pope Pius VI in his constitution "Auctorem Fidei," published on the 28th of August, 1794.[22]

In the nineteenth century the right of the Church in this matter is again emphasized. In the encyclical *"Quanta Cura"* Pope Pius IX directly condemned the proposition that the Church did not possess the right or capability of exercising coercive power.[23] This teaching, which appeared in a book entitled "Juris Ecclesiastici Institutiones Joannis Nepomuceni Nuytz," was specially mentioned by Pius in his letter *"Ad Apostolicae,"* and from this was carried into the "Syllabus of Errors."[24]

Pope Leo XIII in his encyclical "Immortale Dei" vindicated for the Church her right to use coercive measures.[25] Pointing out the exact place to be occupied by the civil power and indicating its proper relation to the spiritual, he says:

> And just as the end at which the Church aims is by far the noblest of ends, so is its authority the most exalted of all authority, nor can it be looked upon as inferior to the civil power, or in any manner dependent upon it.[26]

A little further on he states that there are two powers appointed by God having charge of human affairs, the ecclesiastical and civil; the former being set over divine, the latter over human, things, "so that there is an orbit traced out within which the action of each is brought into play by its own native right."[27]

---

[22] *Fontes,* n. 475; O'Riordan, "Auctorem Fidei," *Catholic Encyclopedia,* II, 68.

[23] 8 dec. 1865—*Fontes,* n. 542.

[24] 22 aug. 1851—*Fontes,* n. 511j, cf. Denzinger-Bannwart, n. 1700, 9.

[25] 1 nov. 1885—*Fontes,* n. 592.

[26] *The Great Encyclical Letters of Leo XIII* (New York, 1903), p. 112.

[27] *Op. cit.,* p. 114.

Throughout the centuries, therefore, the Church has claimed and never surrendered the power granted to her by her Founder, no matter what the errors which were disseminated, no matter how that power was encroached upon by the civil power. From the very beginning upon the death of St. Peter there reigned upon the Fisherman's throne the successor of him to whom Christ addressed his charge: "Feed my lambs, feed my sheep."[28] Reigning over the spiritual, his power is universal, independent and supreme, being subservient to none but God alone.

---

[28] John XXI, 16, 17.

PART ONE

Historical Synopsis

CHAPTER II

Supreme Jurisdiction in the Church

THE POPE

From the earliest centuries the pope has been considered the successor of St. Peter, possessing the full power granted by Christ to this apostle. Not only did he claim the power to serve as the highest court of appeal when there was question of penalties inflicted by other ecclesiastical superiors,[1] but he imposed penalties directly not only upon the laity, but also on the clergy, even upon bishops and metropolitans.

This power flows from the pope's very office, for if he did not possess it he would hold a primacy of honor only. Kober[2] well maintains that the contention of Febronius[3]—that the pope has a penal power only over those directly subject to him as bishop, and not over the subjects of other bishops—cannot be accepted, for primacy without the power to enforce its decrees is incompatible with the office granted by Christ to St. Peter. Early in the history of the Church this power was already exercised. It was recognized by the Council of Sardica (343), for that Council

[1] "Ipsi sunt canones, qui appellationes totius Ecclesiae ad huius sedis examen voluerunt deferre. Ab ipsa vero numquam prorsus appellare debere sanxerunt; ac per hoc illam de tota ecclesia iudicare, ipsam ad nullius conmeare iudicium, nec de eius umquam praeceperunt iudicari iudicio, sententiamque eius constituerunt non oportere dissolui, cuius potius sequenda decreta mandauerunt."—C. 16, C. IX, q. 3; cf. also, cc. 17, 18, C. IX, q. 3.

[2] *Der Kirchenbann nach den Grundsaetzen des canonischen Rechts* (2. ed., Tuebingen, 1863), p. 69.

[3] *De Statu Ecclesiae,* C. II, nn. 11, 12.

declared that if a bishop feels that he has been unjustly deposed, his case may be appealed to the Roman Bishop, and no other bishop was to be elected in his place until the case was submitted to the judgment of the Holy Father.[4] In the dispute that arose over the date of Easter, Pope Victor I threatened with excommunication those Asiatic bishops who would not comply.[5]

In the year 424 the assembled bishops in the synod of Carthage complained to the pope, Celestine, because he had received the appeal of a certain Apiarius, who had been condemned by the synod under the presidency of his metropolitan. They contended that the metropolitan and his council were the authorities to determine such a matter.[6] This, however, seems to have been contrary to the law then existing, for, judging according to the decrees of the Council of Antioch (341), if only a majority decision of condemnation was had, then appeal could be made to a higher authority; if the provincial synod passed a unanimous decision, then further appeal was prohibited.[7] The Council of Sardica (343) permitted a bishop, who had been found guilty by the provincial synod, to make an appeal to the Roman Pontiff, who would then, if necessary, order a new investigation to be made, or permit the previous decision to stand.[8] The objections raised by the bishops at Carthage were rejected in Rome, for

---

[4] C. 3: "Si quis autem episcoporum in aliquo negotio condemnandus visus fuerit, et existimet se non malam, sed bonam causam habere, ut etiam rursus judicium renovetur. . . ."

C. 4: "Si videtur, necesse esse adjici huic sententiae, quam sincera dilectione plenam protulisti, ut si quis episcopus fuerit depositus judicio episcoporum, qui sunt in vicinia et dicat rursus sibi defensionis negotium competere; non prius in cathedram alius substituatur, quam Romanus episcopus causa cognita sententiam tulerit."

C. 5: "Placuit, ut si quis episcopus delatus fuerit, et congregati ejusdem regionis episcopi eum gradu moverint; et veluti appellans confugerit ad beatissimam Romanae ecclesiae episcopum. . . ."—Mansi, III, 7.

[5] Eusebius, *Historia Ecclesiastica* (Scaphusiae, 1862), Lib. V, c. 27.

[6] *Epistola Concilii Africani ad Coelestinum Papam*—Harduin, I, 950.

[7] C. 14, 15—Harduin, I, 599.

[8] Cc. 3, 4, 5—Mansi, III, 7. (The text of these canons is given *supra*, in note 4.)

legislation of traditional standing was contrary to the demand made.

A short time later Pope Innocent I, writing to the bishop of Rouen, declared that if any *causae majores* were submitted to the provincial synod, these were to be examined by the bishops and then submitted to Rome for final examination and adjudication; this, he said, was in conformity with the custom that had grown up in the course of ecclesiastical history.[9]

Just what this term *causae majores* implied at the time is hard to say, yet one sees therein a tendency to limit to the Holy See the final decision in certain, determined matters. The competency of the pope to receive appeals and render final decision was again emphasized by Pope Leo the Great, in his letter to the bishops of the province of Vienne in Gaul, when discussing his action in regard to Hilary of Arles. During the immediately preceding centuries, he wrote, the bishops of the province had frequently consulted and appealed to the Holy See, and it was the constant policy of the Supreme Pontiff in all appeals made to him either to uphold the sentence which the provincial synod had imposed or to reject it as unjust.[10]

In the sixth century Bishop Contumeliosus, who had been deposed by the synod held under Caesarius, the metropolitan of Arles, appealed to Pope Agapitus, declaring his innocence in regard to the accusations against him. In this instance the pope ordered a new trial and advised the metropolitan that instead of carrying out the sentence after an appeal had been made, he should have held it in abeyance until such time as the Holy See had decided the matter.[11]

There was now gradually developing a definite movement to withdraw the infliction of deposition of bishops from the competency of the metropolitan and his synod and to reserve it to the Holy See, classing it among the *causae majores* for which the pope alone was competent. This was the theme of the Pseudo-

---

[9] *Epistola II ad Victricium Rotamagensem*—*MPL*, LVI, 519.

[10] *Epistola X, ad episcopos per provinciam Viennensem constitutos*, c. 2—*MPL*, LIV, 629.

[11] *Agapeti epistola ad Caesarium Arelatensis*—Harduin, II, 1179.

Isidorian decretals and the school of reform that developed as a result. The author of these decretals would grant to the provincial synod merely the power to investigate the charges brought against the bishop. He demanded final adjudication by the Holy See. Whatever may have been the purpose of the author in writing these decretals, he gave voice to a measure now already well on its path of development. Pope Nicholas I (858-867) upheld his papal right, as outlined by his predecessors, to serve as the highest court of appeals,[12] so that these appeals could be made to the Holy See directly without the intervention of an intermediate court.[13] This power he reserved to himself even in the face of great opposition on the part of the Frankish bishops.[14]

In his letter to the bishops of Gaul, Pope Nicholas definitely placed deposition of a bishop in the class of the *causae majores.* If this case is not so to be considered, he wrote, what could be considered greater.[15] Appeals continued to be made to Rome directly, in spite of the decree drawn up at the General Council of Constantinople (869), in which it was specified that a priest may appeal to the metropolitan of the province, who may thereupon summon the suffragans or a *synodus generalis,* and that the bishop may appeal to the patriarch.[16]

Though the popes had spoken clearly as to their power of judging bishops accused of criminal offenses, there continued to be opposition to this reservation especially in France, where various synods persisted in making such judgments. Gradually,

---

[12] C. 10, C. II, q. 1; cf. also, c. 12, C. III, q. 9.

[13] C. 12, C. II, q. 6: "Unde omnium appellantium apostolicam sedem episcoporum judicia, et cuncta maiorum negotia causarum eidem sanctae sedi reservata esse liquet." Cf. also, c. 16, C. II, q. 6.

[14] Synod of Rome (861), *ep. ad Ludovicum II Imperatorem*—Mansi, XV, 598.

[15] Nicolaus I, *Epistola ad universos episcopos Galliae:* "Sed dictis, judicia episcoporum non esse majora negotia nec difficiliores causarum exitus . . . Adhuc tamen percontari libet, quaenam judicia vel quorum esse majora negotia praedicatis, si episcoporum causas non inter praecipua computatis negotia."—Harduin, V, 593.

[16] C. 26—Mansi, XVI, 177; cf. also, *Epistola Hincmari Rhemorum Archiepiscopi ad Hadrianum Papam* (871)—Mansi, XVI, 687.

however, the exclusive competency of the pope was recognized, for he lifted excommunications that had been unrighteously inflicted, and removed bishops unlawfully consecrated and installed.[17] Soon the power of the pope in this matter was expressed to the effect that bishops could not be deposed without the consent of the Holy Father,[18] who must be present either personally or through his legate.[19] Naturally the pope could not attend personally to every case that arose, and frequently he acted through a legate. Thus, in a report of St. Peter Damian, declaration is made of the fact that at a synod convoked in Lyons (1055) Pope Victor II through his legate Hildebrand proceeded to depose six bishops who had been accused and found guilty of various offenses.[20] By the beginning of the twelfth century the reservation of this power was almost everywhere acknowledged, although in a few instances some opposition still appeared.[21]

The Decretals of Gregory IX point to the same reservation. Under Pope Innocent III the power of deposing bishops was exercised directly, either personally or through legates, without

---

[17] Joannes VIII, *ep. CCLXXVI* (ad Romanum Archiepiscopum). In the case here reported, Deusdedit of Ravenna, who was found unjustly excommunicated, was absolved by the pope. The Council of Rome (998), c. 6, prescribed the removal of a certain bishop Stephen, who was unlawfully consecrated and installed—Mansi, XIX, 226. Cf. also the Council of Rheims (975), under Stephen, Legate of Benedict VII, in which the excommunication of Theobaldus, Bishop of Amiens, a usurper, was announced.—Mansi, XIX, 59.

[18] Leo IX, *ep. III* (ad Thomam, Episcopum Africanum) (1054)—Mansi, XIX, 658.

[19] Alexander II, *Fragmenta epistolae* (1053). In this letter the pope condemned one Joselinus, an archdeacon, who obtained the see of Soissons simoniacally, and forbade the consecration until he had justified himself.—Mansi, XIX, 978. At the Council of Winchester (1070), Stigandus of Canterbury was deposed through a legate because he unlawfully occupied that see.—Mansi, XIX, 1079.

[20] Harduin, VI, 1040.

[21] In a Council of the Lateran in 1115, Pope Paschal II settled the dispute that had arisen between Bishops Grosulanus and Jordanus. Grosulanus had been removed, but later restored to his original see. The people refused to accept him and elected Jordanus in his place. Both claimants appeared before this council and presented their case to the Pope for final adjudication.

the assistance of any synod, and as a result this power was claimed as being of divine right and not merely of human or canonical institution; it was pointed out that although a bishop is consecrated by the metropolitan, he may not be condemned by that same metropolitan.[22] This law was finally stated in explicit terms by the Council of Trent, for there it was stated that all criminal cases against bishops, deserving of deposition or deprivation of benefice, are to be judged and decided by the Holy Father alone.[23] If any such case occurs outside the Eternal City, then the case must be transmitted to the Roman Pontiff for final adjudication. Minor criminal offenses were to be considered by the provincial synod alone, by him whom this synod or council has deemed fit to appoint.[24] Although the Council of Trent had legislated in regard to the regular convoking of provincial synods,[25] the practice of convoking them became more and more neglected, and in many places was almost entirely ignored. Under such circumstances the distinction between major and minor offenses could no longer be maintained; hence there soon developed the practice to reserve to the Holy See all criminal cases against bishops without distinction.[26] A subsequent decision by the Congregation of the Council[27] and various encyclical letters of the popes[28] emphasized this same legislation, so that it has remained unaltered from the time of the Council of Trent down to the promulgation of the new Code.

It was not, however, only through the infliction of deposition that the pope exercised his power over bishops, it was used in

---

[22] C. 2, X, *de translatione episcopi,* I, 7.

[23] Sess. XXIV, *de ref.,* c. 5; Sess. XIII, *de ref.,* c. 6.

[24] Sess. XXIV, *de ref.,* c. 5.

[25] Sess. XXIV, *de ref.,* c. 2.

[26] Giraldi, *Expositio Juris Pontificii Juxta Recentiorem Ecclesiae Disciplinam* (Romae, 1829), pp. 559, 1005.

[27] S. C. C., 7 ian. 1623—*Fontes,* n. 2435.

[28] Pius VI, const. *Super soliditate,* 28 nov. 1786, § 14—*Fontes,* n. 473; Gregory XVI, ep. *"Quo ex tuis litteris,"* 24 iul. 1833—*Fontes,* n. 486; Leo XIII, litt. encycl. *"Trans Oceanum,"* 18 apr. 1897—*Fontes,* n. 633.

other ways also. Thus he inflicted excommunication, suspension and other penalties.[29]

The same power was exercised over the laity by the popes in view of their primacy.[30] The exercise of this power manifested itself most frequently in relation to kings, princes and other civil rulers, especially in Catholic nations, for this papal power whenever employed served as a final bulwark of right and justice among a people that was oppressed by an unrelenting sovereign.

Thus, during the course of the centuries the pope was acknowledged as the highest court of appeal; this same appeal was permitted from decisions given directly by their legates or by the councils over which these presided.[31] Further, he was looked upon as the supreme judge of the entire Church.[32] The pope, therefore, held a jurisdiction equal to and superior to that of every other ecclesiastical authority, whether bishop, metropolitan or primate, and could inflict punishments whether in the first instance or as the ultimate court of appeals.

The Council of Trent decreed that all matters that involved litigation should be tried in the first instance before the Ordinary, excepting those cases in which the Holy See alone is competent, or those which the pope by special rescript has reserved to himself.[33] Thus the pope has vindicated to himself the supreme right in these matters of penal affairs, a power which was again acknowledged by the Council of the Vatican (1870) in the Constitution *Pastor aeternus,* in which the pope is spoken of as the one having supreme power over all.[34]

As far as the laity is concerned, this penal power of the pope has but seldom been exercised since the time of the Council of

---

[29] Silvester II, *ep. I* (1001)—Mansi, XIX, 241; Council of Toulouse (1075)—Mansi, XX, 457; Leo IX, *ep. XII* (1050)—Mansi, XIX, 679.

[30] Alexander II, *ep. I* (1001)—Mansi, XIX, 958; John XIII, *ep. ad Alfricum, ducem*—Mansi, XIX, 27; Anastasius IV, *ep. IV, V, VI*—Mansi, XXI, 775.

[31] Urban II (1088-1099), *ep. XXIII* (ad Raynerum S. R. Ecclesiae Presbyterum et Legatum)—Mansi, XX, 679.

[32] C. 20, X, *de foro competenti,* II, 2.

[33] Sess. XXIV, *de ref.,* c. 20.

[34] Sess. IV, c. 3—Denzinger-Bannwart, *Enchiridion Symbolorum,* n. 1868.

Trent. When it was exercised, it was for crimes that because of attendant circumstances were considered unusually grave and serious,[35] or in cases involving individual rulers, and this up to recent times.[36]

---

[35] Innocent X, const. *"Cum sicut,"* 24 mar. 1649—*Bullarium Romanum,* XV, 626; Clement IX, const. *"Cum sicut,"* 26 feb. 1669—*Bullarium Romanum,* XVII, 772; Clement X, const. *"Cum sicut,"* 5 dec. 1672—*Bullarium Romanum,* XVIII, 372.

[36] Clement VIII, const. *"Ex ore,"* 22 dec. 1597—*Bullarium Romanum,* X, 389; Clement VIII, const. *"Divinae gratiae,"* 17 sept. 1895—*Bullarium Romanum,* X, 304; Pius IX, litt. ap. *"Cum Catholica Ecclesia,"* 26 mar. 1860—*Fontes,* n. 528; ep. encycl. *"Respicientes,"* 1 nov. 1870—*Fontes,* n. 559.

CHAPTER III

Participants in the Supreme Jurisdiction in the Church

ARTICLE I. THE PATRIARCH

In the beginning only three patriarchates were recognized, that of Rome, Alexandria and Antioch. Thus the Council of Nicaea (325) decreed that the ancient custom that was in existence in Egypt, namely, that the bishop of Alexandria has the supervision of the provinces of northern Africa, be continued.[1] The same was to be the practice in regard to the bishop of Rome and the bishop of Antioch. These three sees, then, were designated to receive special honor, and with it, any special powers that may be attached thereto. In 381 the Council of Constantinople decreed that the bishop of Constantinople should have the primacy of honor after the bishop of Rome, because it was the new Rome.[2] The pope then reigning as well as his successors refused to accept this canon, thereby denying the validity of the claim made to the patriarchal honor. In 451 the Council of Chalcedon established Constantinople as a patriarchate, an action that was refused recognition by Pope Leo the Great because this measure was passed in the absence of his legate. At length, however, the desires of Constantinople were granted. It was the VIII General Council of Constantinople (869), that solemnly affirmed the position of the five patriarchates, placing Constantinople second only to Rome.[3] Jerusalem, too, was elevated to the patriarchate.

The rights of the patriarch over the metropolitan and bishops residing in his territory were very limited. To him was given

[1] C. 6—Harduin, I, 323.

[2] C. 3—Harduin, I, 809.

[3] C. 21—Harduin, V, 909; cf. also Schroeder, *Disciplinary Decrees of the General Councils* (London and St. Louis: Herder, 1937), 246, where there is given the 5th canon of the IV General Council of the Lateran (1215), which confirmed canon 21 of the IV General Council of Constantinople (869).

the right to consecrate the metropolitan and also the bishops with the permission of the immediate superior metropolitan. Further, he was permitted to assemble the metropolitans and individual bishops in synod, over which he himself presided.[4] In the beginning he also had the right to judge individual metropolitans, even to proceed to the infliction of penalties. Whether or not this could be done directly or only together with the synod is questionable, but it is more probable that individual action was forbidden. Kober points out that in the beginning it was the practice of the Church that all major cases, among which deposition of a bishop must be considered, was reserved to the provincial synod; hence, he concludes, the same practice must have applied to the patriarch in regard to subordinate metropolitans.[5] Bouix, without hesitation, expresses it as his opinion that the patriarch could never sit in judgment in any case involving a metropolitan without first having convoked his council.[6]

Greater coercive power than this, however, the patriarch never gained according to ecclesiastical law. As a final and definite measure, the rights of the patriarchs in the West were summed up in the Constitution of Benedict XIV, "*Apostolica,*" issued in 1742. The rights herein granted were: 1) to summon and preside at the patriarchal synods, whose acts must be confirmed by Rome; 2) to ordain all bishops of their territory and to consecrate the sacred chrism; 3) to receive appeals made against judgments of the metropolitans. Upon them was imposed the obligation of making a visitation of their patriarchate every third year.[7]

Thus the Latin patriarch has from the beginning enjoyed honors that were not granted to the metropolitans who were subordinated to him. There were not, however, given to him any penal powers that he could exercise directly, for in the exercise of any such

[4] Council of Chalcedon (451), c. 17—Harduin, II, 607; IV Council of Constantinople (869), c. 26—Harduin, V, 909.

[5] *Deposition und Degradation nach den Grundsaetzen des kirchlichen Rechts* (Tuebingen, 1867), p. 499.

[6] *Tractatus de Episcopo ubi et de Synodo Dioecesana* (2. ed., 2 vols., Parisii, 1873), I, 428.

[7] Feb. 14, 1742—*Bullarii Romani Continuatio,* I, 140.

measures he was always dependent upon the synod which he had convoked.

ARTICLE II. THE METROPOLITAN

As early as the fourth century mention is made of the metropolitan, whose office was that of superior to a group of individual bishops. The metropolitan lived in the city which was prominent both civilly and ecclesiastically; it is from this circumstance that his name of Metropolitan was derived.[8]

The office of the metropolitan is not one that has its source in the divine law, *ius divinum,* as has the papacy and episcopacy, but is one that has developed through the course of the centuries and is of purely ecclesiastical, and for that reason, human origin.[9] It participates, not in the episcopal power of the individual bishop, but in the primatial power of the pope. The power of the metropolitan over his suffragans, as far as the canons have granted it, partakes in a certain sense of that of a *iudex ordinarius* over the bishops belonging to the province; thus he is spoken of in the Decretals in the *Corpus Iuris Canonici.*[10] Barbosa[11] and Reiffenstuel,[12] discussing the power that the metropolitan has in the diocese of a suffragan when there is evident negligence on the

---

[8] Though at first the term *metropolitan* had a distinctive and exclusive meaning, it gradually became synonymous with that of *archbishop,* one who was placed at the head of a province, having several suffragan bishops under him. Thus, hereafter, these offices will be considered as synonymous, both being subject to the same rules drawn up for the guidance of the bishop at the head of the province.

[9] Thomassinus, *Vetus et Nova Ecclesiae Disciplina* (Moguntiaci, 1787), Pars I, Lib. I, cap. XXVI, n. 5: "Ex quo id efficitur, quod . . . Metropolitanas quascumque dignitates posterior Ecclesiae foecunditas creavit, inter Pontificem summum et Episcopos quoscumque medias, aut imitationes et imagines, aut emanationes et veluti rivulos esse privilegii Petri." Hereafter this work will be referred to as *Thomassinus.* Cf. also, Phillips, *Kirchenrecht* (3. ed., 7 vols., Regensburg, 1855-1869), II, 82; "nicht *divinae institutionis,* sondern *humanae constitutionis.*"

[10] C. 11, X, *de officio iudicis ordinarii,* I, 31.

[11] *De officio et potestate episcopi* (Lugduni, 1656), Pars III, Allegatio 126, n. 6.

[12] *Ius Canonicum Universum* (5 vols. in 7, Parisiis, 1864-1870), Lib. I, Tit. X, n. 10.

part of that suffragan, are of the opinion that any jurisdiction that he may have in such a case is based, not on a *potestas ordinaria,* but on a concession of the law.

In the early Church it was the metropolitan who had the right to convoke and preside over the provincial synod,[13] at which, among other things, investigation was made of the justice and legitimacy of the penalties imposed by the individual bishops or mitigated by them, no matter whether these penalties were imposed upon priests, deacons and other members of the clergy, or upon any member of the laity.[14]

During these first centuries this right to preside over the provincial synod was the extent of the power of the metropolitan as far as penal measures are concerned.[15] Pope Calixtus I (217-222) wrote that metropolitans should not presume to excommunicate or to judge any one subject to one of his suffragan bishops without first having consulted that same bishop.[16] He then goes on to say that if the metropolitan proceeds in any way in the diocesan affairs of a suffragan without having consulted the latter, all acts shall be invalid.

In the following centuries, however, the metropolitan began to secure more power over the province. In the XI Council of Toledo (675) it was decreed that throughout the province the same method of reciting and carrying out the divine office should be observed. A violator of this law was to be deprived of communion with the faithful for six months, being subject to the metropolitan for proper correction during this time. This law bound not merely the clerics and priests of the province, but even the bishops.[17]

---

[13] Council of Antioch (341), c. 16—Harduin, I, 599; Council of Chalcedon (451), c. 19—Harduin, II, 609.

[14] Council of Antioch (341), cc. 6, 9, 14—Harduin, I, 595, 597, 599; Council of Nicaea (325), cc. 4, 5—Harduin, I, 323.

[15] Hinschius, *System des katholischen Kirchenrechts* (4 vols., Berlin, 1869-1888), II, 2.

[16] *Ep. II*—Harduin, I, 111.

[17] C. 3: "... placuit huic concilio, ut metropolitanae sedis auctoritate coacti uniuscujusque provinciae pontifices, rectoresque ecclesiarum, unum eumdemque in psallendo teneant modum, quem in metropolitana sede cognoverint

The Council of Meaux, in the year 845, made this concession to the metropolitan, that a sentence of anathema, total exclusion from the Church and condemnation to perdition, should be pronounced on no one without the consultation and approval of this superior.[18]

In the ninth century there arose in the West a conflict that went a long way in determining that it was the pope who had the right to pass upon those cases which involved a bishop, for which the punishment to be inflicted was that of deposition.[19] The outstanding case in this connection is that in which Hincmar, metropolitan of Rheims, deposed Rothad of Soissons, and consecrated another in his place. Rothad had been deprived of his see at a synod at which he was not present, and in spite of an appeal that he made to the pope. In the course of the proceedings that preceded the final settlement of the case, Pope Nicholas I threatened the Archbishop with canonical penalties.[20] Writing to the Frankish bishops Pope Nicholas replied to the charge that Rothad did not have a just cause for making an appeal, a charge which they had based upon the canons of the Council of Sardica (343)[21] which demanded a *bona causa*. The answer was that Bishop Rothad felt that he had such a cause and this sufficed for an appeal. In a letter to Hincmar, the pope pointed out that in the future deposition proceedings against any bishop could be carried

---

institutum; nec aliqua diversitate cujusque ordinis, vel officii a metropolitana se patiantur sede disjungi. Abbatibus sane indultis officiis quae juxta voluntatem sui episcopi regulariter illis implenda sunt, cetera officia publica, id est, vesperam, matutinum, sive Missam, aliter quam in principali ecclesia celebrare non liceat. Quisquis horum decretorum violator exstiterit, sex mensibus communione privatus, apud metropolitanum sub poenitentiae censura permaneat corrigendus; qualiter apud illum, et praeteritae transgressionis culpam lacrymis diluat, et necessariam officiorum doctrinam addiscat. Sub ista regula disciplinae, non solum metropolitanus totius provinciae pontifices vel sacerdotes adstringat, sed etiam ceteri episcopi subjectos sibi ecclesiarum rectores his obtemperare institutionibus cogant."—Harduin, III, 1024.

[18] C. 56—Harduin, IV, 1493.

[19] Mansi, XV, 285 sq.; Hefele, *Konciliengeschichte* (2. ed., 9 vols., 1873-1890), II, 62.

[20] Mansi, XV, 295.

[21] Canons 3, 4, 5—Mansi, III, 7. (For the wording of these canons, see note 4 of chapter II.)

out only with the approval of the Holy Father. The metropolitan was now given an alternative of abiding by the sentence or of coming to Rome together with Rothad and presenting his case; in the meantime Rothad was to be permitted to return to his diocese.[22] If neither the one nor the other was done, a perpetual and complete suspension would be imposed upon the metropolitan.

Looking at the Decretals of the *Corpus Iuris Canonici,* one finds that an archbishop as metropolitan was given certain rights and duties, involving some penal and coercive powers over his suffragans and their subjects, powers which are definitely stated. Pope Innocent III pointed out that no prelate, whether patriarch, primate or metropolitan, had any more rights than the bishop had in his own diocese, unless these were granted by the canons themselves, or by legitimate and ancient custom.[23] The metropolitan, however, was given the right to receive appeals from the subjects of his suffragans; he could not, however, enter at will into a dispute arising in the diocese of the suffragan; appeal had to be made in the proper legal manner.[24] The same pope, answering an inquiry of the metropolitan of Paris, stated that, if it became notorious that a penalty imposed upon a subject by a suffragan was evidently unjust and indiscreet, he, in view of his metropolitan authority, might declare that the subject was unreasonably censured.[25] Finally, the metropolitan had the right to impose an excommunication upon the vicar of his suffragan, but this for a reasonable cause only.[26] The Glossators tell us what constitutes such a reasonable cause.[27] The metropolitan may act if the appointee of the suffragan is remiss in the office entrusted to him, or in the proper use of the jurisdiction that is his in virtue of his office; if, however, this appointee acts as a private individual and not in virtue of his office, then the metropolitan has no power over him. This appointee is further liable to correction and punishment at the hands of the metropoli-

[22] Nicholas I, *Epistola ad Hincmar*—Mansi, XV, 691.

[23] C. 9, X, *de officio iudicis ordinarii,* I, 31.

[24] C. 1, X, *de officio legati,* I, 30.

[25] C. 54, X, *de appellationibus,* II, 28.

[26] C. 1, *de officio vicarii,* I, 13, in VI°.

[27] Cf. *glossa* to *rationabili causa* in c. 1, *de officio vicarii,* I, 13, in VI°.

tan if he interferes in any way so as to hinder the making of an appeal from the suffragan to the metropolitan, or if he performs any act of jurisdiction while his own bishop is under censure.

Over the suffragans themselves the metropolitan was also given certain well-defined powers. A question was presented to Pope Innocent III in 1204, asking whether a suffragan bishop may be delegated to adjudicate an appeal that had been presented to the metropolitan; and it was further asked, if the suffragan could be forced to accept if he refused the delegation. In response the pope pointed out that a metropolitan could not force an unwilling suffragan to accept such a delegation, since he had no jurisdiction over that suffragan except in certain cases.[28] Here again the Glossators are of assistance, for they show what these exceptional cases are. The first is when there is an evident departure in the celebration of the divine office from the custom and method of the metropolitan church; this right was of long standing, having been granted by the XI Council of Toledo in the seventh century.[29] Should the suffragan be guilty of the commission of a crime within the diocese over which the metropolitan rules, he would be liable to punishment at the hands of the metropolitan. Further, if the suffragan possessed any estate or property within the confines of the metropolitan see, this possession would be governed by the same rules and laws as that of any other subject of that see. Finally, if a criminal case arose in which the parties were a suffragan and one of his own subjects such a case came under the jurisdiction of the metropolitan.[30]

There was also given to the metropolitan a penal power that has continued even to the present time. If any notorious crimes were committed against the metropolitan or those under his charge and care at the time of his canonical visitation or on the occasion of the convocation of a provincial council, so as to impede his jurisdiction in any way, then he was permitted to proceed against the guilty one, and to impose fitting penalties. Pope Innocent IV (1243-1254) went on to extend this power

[28] C. 11, X, *de officio iudicis ordinarii,* I, 31.
[29] Cf. note 17 of this section.
[30] Cf. *glossa* to *exceptis* in c. 11, X, *de officio iudicis ordinarii,* I, 31.

even to those who were the cause of any sort of injury or offense, even though it did not interfere with the metropolitan's jurisdiction.[31] While making this visitation, the metropolitan was permitted to punish any crime or delict that was notorious and which did not demand examination, provided that that crime was left unpunished due to the ordinary's neglect; otherwise the matter was to be called to the attention of the bishop, who was thereafter to proceed with the case.[32] Any other jurisdiction that the metropolitan could legitimately exercise on such a visitation could find its justification in custom only.[33]

The Council of Trent upheld the metropolitan's right of canonical visitation, but specified these conditions, namely, that the metropolitan had previously made a proper visitation of his own diocese as the ancient canons demanded,[34] and, in addition, that he had received the approval of the provincial synod.[35] Further, the infliction of lesser penalties was also made dependent on the cooperation of the provincial synod.[36] It was not permitted to the metropolitan to inflict a suspension or excommunication without the approval of the synod,[37] with the exception of those cases in which the metropolitan was impeded during the time of the visitation, or in which he simply declared a penalty that had already been inflicted *ipso jure*.[38]

Hence, after the time of the Council of Trent, the metropolitan was deprived of many of his former powers over his suffragans and their subjects. The office became one almost wholly devoid of any penal powers, that is powers that were to be exercised by him not merely as a bishop or archbishop, but precisely as a metropolitan.

---

[31] C. 1, *de poenis*, V, 9, in VI°.

[32] C. 1, *de censibus*, III, 20, in VI°.

[33] Gonzalez-Tellez, *Commentaria Perpetua in Singulos Textus Quinque Librorum Decretalium Gregorii* IX (5 vols. in 4, Lugduni, 1715), Lib. I, Tit. XXXI, cap. 9.

[34] C. 25, X, *de censibus*, III, 39; c. 1, *de censibus*, III, 20, in VI°.

[35] Sess. XXIV, *de ref.*, c. 3.

[36] Sess. XXIV, *de ref.*, c. 5.

[37] Kober, *Die Suspension der Kirchendiener* (Tuebingen, 1862), p. 40.

[38] Kober, *Der Kirchenbann*, p. 70.

ARTICLE III. VICARS AND PREFECTS APOSTOLIC, ABBOTS AND PRELATES *Nullius*

In the territory assigned them, Vicars and Prefects Apostolic, Abbots and Prelates *Nullius* possess the same power in criminal affairs as do the bishops in their respective dioceses. Not enjoying true episcopal jurisdiction, these ecclesiastical superiors do not participate in the episcopal jurisdiction in the Church, but in the supreme jurisdiction. Since, however, it is not the purpose of this work to consider these offices in themselves but merely in the coercive powers they possess, no special treatment will be given here. Their rights and powers will be considered in union with those of the bishop, and the bishop's rights and powers will be considered forthwith.

CHAPTER IV

Episcopal Jurisdiction in the Church

THE BISHOP

Already in apostolic times, when among the faithful some were excluded from participation in ecclesiastical functions because of specified major offenses, we find the basis of a definite penal system that was to develop gradually through the centuries of ecclesiastical history. The care of the religious and moral welfare of the faithful was placed, from the beginning, in the hands of the bishop, for to him was given the power which had been bestowed by Christ upon His apostles.[1] In apostolic times no definite system of imposing penal measures existed; the Church was still in its infancy and as yet was unable to enact universal regulations which demanded the experience of years to perfect.

In post-apostolic times, with the spread of Christianity throughout the then known world, and the more determinate organization of the communities and churches, definite measures were adopted. It is true that St. Cyprian refers to the consultation of priests before acting;[2] still one is not justified in concluding that he therefore felt that such approval was necessary for validity, for elsewhere he speaks differently, and his meeting with other bishops in council to settle matters of discipline shows that he felt that these things could be judged directly. The practice, handed down from the apostolic period, that only mortal or capital sins merited total rejection or excommunication,[3] was still in vogue in the fourth century.[4] There was no definite rule, however,

[1] I Cor. V, 2-4; II Thess. III, 14.

[2] *Ep. XIV—MPL,* IV, 261.

[3] In the early Church the terminology was very general. The word "excommunication" included all penalties and inferred the meaning that "the one penalized had been placed outside of the communion to which his grade in the Church entitled him, either wholly or in part."—Gans, "Censure," *Catholic Encyclopedia,* III, 528.

[4] Cc. 21, 22, C. XI, q. 3.

as to which sins were to be included in this category, and the administration of penal and coercive measures was left, to a great extent, to the determination and decision of the individual bishops. Imposition of excommunication, however, as far as it can be ascertained, was not dependent on the fact that the commission of the crime was notorious; nevertheless, it was necessary that its commission be established as a fact in the estimation of the superior.[5]

It was not only the laity, however, which was subject to the penal powers of the Church. The clergy also came under its jurisdiction, for as early as the third century one reads of excommunication, deposition, and the deprivation of income imposed upon refractory members of the clergy.[6] Even bishops who were known as *lapsi* were treated in a manner similar to that of the laity before reconciliation was effected.[7]

It has been stated above that during the first centuries, while the Church was confronted with rapid spread and frequent persecution, no definite penal system had been universally adopted. Once freedom was granted by the Empire, the Church was confronted with new problems. The gradual elimination of the strict laws that practically isolated early Christian and non-Christian and the marked growth that followed upon the conversion of the Emperor—these were factors that made the transgressions of ecclesiastical laws more numerous. The need of a more definite penal system was evident, especially in view of the fact that the old severity in regard to excommunication from the body of the faithful was gradually relaxed.

As in the preceding period so also now it was the bishop who exercised penal powers over the faithful. Still it was the custom for the bishop to seek outside counsel, or at least to hear his priests and deacons.[8] He was enabled to exercise his power in three cases:

---

[5] Augustinus, *Sermo* CCCLI, c. 10—*MPL,* XXXIX, 1546.

[6] Cyprianus, *ep. LXV—MPL,* IV, 393; *ep. XXVIII—MPL,* IV, 300.

[7] Cyprianus, *ep. LXIV—MPL,* IV, 389.

[8] IV Council of Carthage (398), c. 23—Harduin, I, 980; cf. also Reiffenstuel, Lib. III, tit. IX, n. 23.

1. When an accusation was made before him, by one worthy of credence, a fact that was determined through a preliminary investigation;[9]
2. when the guilty party, prompted by a desire to undertake the required penance, presented himself and admitted his guilt;[10]
3. when the fault had become notorious, so that it was evident to all that a certain person was unquestionably guilty.[11]

The regulations concerning the investigation and examination of the accusing and the accused;[12] the value of the proof offered,[13] and the issuance of the decree by the bishop, all point to the conclusion that the exercise of the penal powers of the bishop alone was involved. Inasmuch as only a few sins were considered and classed as capital sins or crimes in the eyes of the Church, it was left to a great extent to the judgment of the bishop to determine what penances were to be applied in the case of lesser offences.

The practice of giving several admonitions before the imposition of penalties was to be effected had its source in the words of Christ, for He said that then only was one to be considered as a heathen and publican when he remained adamant in spite of threefold admonitions.[14] A similar advice was given to Titus by St. Paul.[15]

Although there are decrees which recommend the use of such

---

[9] C. 49, C. II, q. 7: "Clericos aut laicos accusantes Episcopos, aut clericos passim, et sine probatione, ad accusationem non recipiendos decernimus, nisi prius eorum discutiatur existimationis opinio."

[10] C. 18, C. II, q. 1: "Nos a communione prohibere quemquam non possumus nisi aut sponte confessum, aut in aliquo, sive saeculari, sive Ecclesiastico judicio nominatum atque convictum."

[11] C. 19, C. XXIII, q. 4; c. 15, C. II, q. 1: "Manifesta accusatione non indigent."

[12] C. 11, C. XXIII, q. 4; Council of Arles (314), c. 14—Harduin, I, 265.

[13] IV Council of Carthage (398), c. 58—Harduin, I, 980.

[14] Matth. XVIII, 16, 17.

[15] Tit. III, 10.

admonitions,[16] and other records which show their application,[17] one cannot say that it was prescribed or obligatory on every occasion. The necessity of these admonitions may easily have depended on the punishment to be inflicted, or on the fact whether the commission of the crime was attended with circumstances or the giving of scandal to such an extent that it was thereby given the character of exceptional gravity. At times the end sought might have been the reform of the guilty, whereas on other occasions the end in view was punishment for a wrong committed.[18]

Mention of the imposition of penalties immediately, i.e., without preceding admonitions, presents the question of the existence of *censurae* or *poenae latae sententiae.* Among the more modern proponents of the school which holds that such measures did not exist are Hinschius[19] and Boehmer.[20] They base their claim on the words of Van Espen, who contends that during the first ten centuries this kind of excommunication was unknown. He expresses serious doubts that even one instance of an *"excommunicatio latae sententiae"* could be found in the *Decretum* of Gratian.[21]

---

[16] C. 15, C. XXIV, q. 3: I Council of Clermont (535), c. 14—Harduin, II, 1182; IV Council of Orleans (541), cc. 15, 25—Harduin, II, 1439; III Council of Paris (557), c. 1—Harduin, III, 337; II Council of Tours (567), cc. 24, 25—Harduin, III, 366; I Council of Rheims (624), cc. 2, 14, 17—Harduin, III, 571.

[17] Council of Ephesus (431)—Harduin, I, 1441; Council of Chalcedon (451)—Harduin, II, 340, 377.

[18] Council of Elvira (305), c. 52—Harduin, I, 255.

[19] *Kirchenrecht,* IV, 761.

[20] *Jus Ecclesiasticum Protestantium* (Magdeburg, 1774), Lib. III, Cap. XLI, § 46; Lib. V, Cap. XXXIX, § 58.

[21] *Jus Ecclesiasticum Universum Ceteraque Scripta Omnia* (5 vols., Venetiis, 1769), P. III, tit. XI, c. 7, nn. 19, 20; "Quidquid sit de hac Gersonii solutione et expositione, hoc sat constat, quod per decem facile saecula ignota fuerit haec species excommunicationis, ita ut in Canonibus paulo antiquioribus nunquam legantur haec aut similia verba: 'Sit ipso facto excommunicatus, qui id fecerit, ipso jure excommunicationem incurrat'; sed tantum 'si quis id fecerit, excommunicetur, deponatur, etc.' quibus consentiunt Canonistae et Theologi, non exprimitur excommunicatio latae

It is true, as Van Espen points out, that it is most difficult to find any citation among the canons of the early Church which contains the words *"ipso facto"* and other similar terms, but the principle implied by these words is found in various councils.[22]

From the wording of these laws, Kober claims, it is evident that this penalty is not one that shall follow merely upon the condemnation and sentence of the superior, but one that shall be suffered for even secret crimes of this nature. While not using the terminology that would be used at present, the canons of these councils certainly express the principle of the *"ipso facto"* incurred excommunication or penalty.[23]

As in the first three centuries[24] so now the bishop continued to be the immediate superior who exercised penal jurisdiction over the clergy of his church and diocese. The Council of Antioch (341) makes clear mention of deposition as being imposed upon a priest or deacon by his bishop,[25] while the Council of Sardica (343) also makes express mention of the bishop's penal powers.[26] Pope Gregory the Great (590-604) furthermore spoke of this power when writing to the bishop of Palermo, telling him that when any report of misconduct among his clerics is brought to his attention, he should make a proper investigation and ascertain the truth of the charges in the presence of the "elders"[27] and then proceed to the application of the canonical measures as the

---

sententiae, sed ferendae duntaxat. Si Decretum Gratiani revolvatur, . . . nescio utrum vel una reperitur excommunicatio latae sententiae."

[22] Council of Vernon (755), c. 9: "Si quis presbyter ab episcopo suo degradatus fuerit, et ipse per contemptum postea aliquid de suo officio sine commeatu facere praesumpserit, et postea . . . excommunicatus fuerit; qui cum ipso communicaverit scienter, sciat se esse excommunicatum. Similiter quicumque clericus, aut laicus, vel femina incestum commiserit, et ab episcopo suo excommunicatus fuerit; si quis cum ipso communicaverit scienter, sciat se excommunicatum esse."—Harduin, III, 1996. Cf. also, IV Council of Toledo (633), c. 75—Harduin, III, 593.

[23] *Der Kirchenbann,* p. 54; Hollweck, *Die Kirchlichen Strafgesetze* (Mainz, 1889), p. 87, nota 2.

[24] Cf. pg.

[25] C. 4—Harduin, I, 595.

[26] C. 7—Harduin, I, 642.

[27] The Glossators tell us that these are the canons.

fault demands.[28] Scandal and extreme gravity alone justified a superior to inflict punishment without following the ordinary procedure, for the Council of Agde (506) reminded the bishops that they must proceed with "sacerdotal moderation," lest they presume to condemn, even excommunicate, the innocent or those not wholly culpable.[29]

To avoid giving scandal and to promote the edification and sanctification of the faithful, various popes and councils recommended to the bishops that those of the clergy who had been accused of or had been found guilty of crime, even though many years had elapsed, were to be prohibited from the celebration of the Holy Sacrifice until such time as would be deemed proper by the bishop.[30] The Council of Lerida (524) decreed in a similar fashion, recommending that a priest who had slain a man in self-defense should refrain from fulfilling his office for a period of two years. During this time he should expiate his deed by prayer, fasts, vigils and alms.[31]

Early in the history of the Church are found laws which remind the bishops that their powers are not universal, but are restricted to those who are their subjects.[32] The Council of Nismes (394) stated that no bishop should undertake to inflict any punishment on a cleric of another diocese without having previously consulted the cleric's immediate superior.[33] This principle of jurisdiction

---

[28] C. 2, C. XV, q. 7; C. 23, D. LXXVI: "Si quid de quocumque clerico ad aures tuas pervenerit, quod te iuste possit offendere; facile non credas, nec ad vindictam te res accendat incognita; sed praesentibus Ecclesiae tuae Senioribus diligenter veritas est perscrutanda, et tunc, si qualitas rei poposcerit, canonica districtio culpam feriat delinquentis." (The two citations, from Gratian's *Decretum* though varying slightly in terminology, are substantially identical in meaning.)

[29] C. 3—Harduin, II, 998.

[30] Rainer, *Suspension of Clerics* (The Catholic University of America, Canon Law Studies, n. 111, Washington, D. C.: The Catholic University of America, 1937), p. 12.

[31] C. 1—Harduin, II, 1065.

[32] C. 1, C. IX, q. 2; c. 3, C. IX, q. 2; I Council of Constantinople (381), c. 2—Harduin, I, 809; II Council of Carthage (390), c. 11—Harduin, I, 953; Council of Tours (461), c. 9—Harduin, II, 795.

[33] C. 4—Hefele, *Conciliengeschichte* (9 vols., Vols. VIII and IX by Hergenroether, Freiburg im Breisgau, 1873-1890), II, 62.

over a determined territory and over determined subjects, once it was established, continued on through the centuries. In a response to one of the bishops of Britain, Pope Gregory the Great stated that it was not fitting for one to judge a person subject to another, but, rather, good should be effected through admonitions and persuasion.[34]

In certain instances, however, especially when the common good or the particular circumstances demanded it, action was seemingly taken in opposition to this policy, for the Council of Compiegne (757) advised that a bishop should not be unduly disturbed if one of his subjects was censured by the bishop of another diocese for crimes that had been committed there.[35] This distinction was again mentioned in a response of Innocent III, when he replied to the bishop of Sienna, who had asked which bishop had the right to judge and pass sentence in the case in which a cleric committed a crime entailing deprivation of benefice in a diocese where he had a patrimonial domicile, while at the same time he held a benefice which demanded residence in another diocese. In answer to this question the pope replied that it was the bishop in whose diocese the crime was committed who was to pass sentence; it was, however, the bishop in whose diocese the benefice existed who was to execute the sentence.[36]

This penal power solely over one's own subjects was again specified by the Council of Trent, when it legislated that a bishop should not proceed against a cleric who was not his own subject, no matter how serious the offense, without first having contacted the proper bishop; and this under pain of invalidity.[37]

Although there was no further development in the penal powers of the bishop during the centuries immediately preceding the Council of Trent, this power was frequently upheld and emphasized. Pope Gregory the Great frequently pointed out just what the bishop's powers were.[38] In the Decretals in the *Corpus Iuris*

---

[34] C. 1, C. VI, q. 3.

[35] *Monumenta Germaniae Historica, Leges* (5 vols., I-IV ed. Pertz; V, ed. Pertz-Waitz-Brunner, Hanover, 1835-1889), I, 552.

[36] C. 14, X, *de foro competenti,* II, 2.

[37] Sess. XIV, *de ref.,* c. 8.

[38] *Epistolae,* Lib. IX, 32, and Lib. XII, 13—Mansi, X, 270, 392.

Canonici mention is made of this same power. Thus, in a synod held under Pope John VIII in 872, it was pointed out that bishops have the power to investigate, judge and punish crimes that were committed within their jurisdiction.[39] The IV General Council of the Lateran (1215) was most emphatic in attributing this power to the bishop.[40] In the Council of Vienne (1311) attention was called to the crimes, sometimes enormous, which were being committed by some of the clergy. The Council noted that such actions were not only bringing disrepute upon the Church, but were the cause of scandals among the people, and yet many bishops were letting such abuses go unheeded.[41] Finally the Council of Trent summed up, in a certain sense, the legislation that had preceded. All of the secular clergy, no matter of what position or rank, as well as regulars when outside their monastery, were subject to the ordinary of the diocese in all matters of discipline. He could proceed against them in conformity with canonical prescriptions whenever there was need of punishment and correction.[42] The right and duty to proceed was not confined merely to the time of the visitation, when the ordinary was to take special cognizance of affairs, but the sanction of his authority obtained even at times other than those of his canonical visitation,[43] in short, the ordinary was rightfully authorized to intervene whenever and as often as there was need of penal procedure.[44]

---

[39] C. 1, X, *de officio iudicis ordinarii,* I, 31.

[40] C. 7: "Irrefragabili constitutione sancimus, ut ecclesiarum praelati ad corrigendum subditorum excessus, maxime clericorum, et reformandos mores prudenter ac diligenter intendant, ne sanguis eorum de suis manibus requiratur. Ut autem correctionis et reformationis officium libere valeant exercere, decernimus, ut executionem ipsorum nulla consuetudo vel appellatio valeat impedire, nisi formam in talibus excesserint observandam."—Harduin, VIII, 25.

[41] C. 1, *de officio iudicis ordinarii,* I, 9, in Clem.: ". . . eisdem episcopis districte iniungimus, quatenus sic circa correctionem clericorum huiusmodi vigilanter intendant, et diligenter sui officii debitum exsequantur, quod et iidem clerici metu poenae, a suis arceantur insolentiis, et alii eorum exemplo perterriti, prosilire ad similia merite pertimescant."

[42] Sess. VI, *de ref.,* c. 3.

[43] Sess. XXIV, *de ref.,* c. 10.

[44] Sess. XIV, *de. ref.,* c. 4.

Although this penal and disciplinary power was always conceded to the bishops as a power that was theirs in view of the office they held, they were not permitted to exercise it in a purely arbitrary manner. It was deemed a dictate of natural justice that a due and commensurate proportion had to exist between the crime or fault and its merited penalty. Hence it was that various councils emphatically pointed out that for the imposition of grave penalties there had to be manifest the commission of a serious offense.[45] This legislation did not remain merely a matter of local observance, for the laws enacted at these councils soon became the law of the entire Church.[46] In all these matters touching upon the infliction of penalties there could of course be no hard and fast rule, nor any system that could serve as an absolute criterion; much was left to the judgment of the bishop exercising his office in the individual case, for all circumstances and conditions, both local and personal, were to be considered.[47] There were certain laws, however, which advised the use of extreme measures, such as suspension and excommunication, as a last resort only;[48] such legislation naturally implied that it was only after other measures had been tried in vain that extremes were at all to be considered. To guard against all possible malfeasance the Councils of Cologne (1536)[49] and Mayence (1549),[50] and finally the Council of Trent, pointed out what the canonical practice should be in respect to penalties righteously inflicted.[51]

---

[45] V Council of Orleans (549), c. 2—Harduin, II, 1444; Council of Meaux (845), c. 56—Harduin, IV, 1493.

[46] Cc. 8, 41, 42, C. XI, q. 3; c. 48, X, *de sententia excommunicationis*, V, 39.

[47] Benedict XIV, *De Synodo Dioecesana* (Romae, 1806), Lib. X, cap. 3, n. 5: "Ex quibus omnibus conficitur, impossibile esse, ut episcopis certa praescribatur norma, ad quam tuto et sine offendiculo conformare se queant in decernendis censuris latae sententiae, cum res pendeat a rerum, locorum et temporum conditionibus, quas perpendere ad ipsorum prudentiam pertinet."

[48] C. 2, C. V, q. 2; c. 8, X, *de dolo et contumacia*, II, 14; c. 2, X, *de testibus cogendis*, II, 21.

[49] Pars XIII, c. 5—Harduin, IX, 2025.

[50] C. 103—Harduin, IX, 2139.

[51] Sess. XXV, *de ref.*, c. 3. A similar pertinent text of the conciliar decrees of the Council of Trent now is incorporated in canon 2214, § 2.

Still further to assure the administration of justice, the policy of giving the canonical admonition, which existed already in the first centuries of the Church,[52] was carried on into the Middle Ages and beyond. The III General Council of the Lateran (1179) included this procedure among its decrees.[53] This legislation was soon extended to the entire Church, for it was embodied in the *Corpus Iuris Canonici* together with other legislation treating of the giving of admonitions before imposing penalties.[54]

The Fathers of the Council of Trent granted to the bishops a further and more drastic power, a power which the needs of the time undoubtedly demanded. It was the power whereby bishops were enabled with completely unchallengeable authority to bar unworthy candidates from the reception of orders and to suspend incriminated clerics from the exercise of their orders already received. In the use of this power they could proceed extra-judicially, that is, upon a simple, certified, personal knowledge that this drastic intervention was justified.[55]

It was at this time that religious disturbance was rife, for it was the period following immediately upon the so-called reformation of Luther. The spiritual life of the clergy had been gradually declining; scandals were numerous; the commission of crimes was frequent. It was under such circumstances that the Council passed its legislation.[56] This legislation connoted at one and the

---

[52] Earlier legislation is cited in note 16 of this chapter.

[53] C. 6: "Reprehensibilis valde consuetudo in quibusdam partibus inolevit, ut fratres et coepiscopi nostri, seu etiam archidiaconi, quos appellaturos in causis suis existimant, nulla penitus admonitione praemissa suspensionis vel excommunicationis in eos ferant sententiam. . . . Quocirca praesenti decreto statuimus, ut nec praelati, nisi canonica commonitione praemissa, suspensionis vel excommunicationis sententiam proferant in subjectos."—Harduin, VII, 1676.

[54] C. 14, X, *de vita et honestate clericorum,* III, 1; cc. 4, 6, X, *de cohabitatione clericorum,* III, 2; c. 13, *de sententia excommunicationis,* V, 11, in VI°.

[55] Cf. Murphy, *Suspension ex Informata Conscientia* (The Catholic University of America, Canon Law Studies, n. 76, Washington, D. C.: The Catholic University of America, 1932), p. 1 sq.

[56] Sess. XIV, *de ref.,* c. 1: "Cum honestius ac tutius sit subjecto debitam praepositis obedientiam impendendo in inferiori ministerio deservire, quam

same time a return to the ancient discipline of the Church and a sanction through positive law for the power thus bestowed.

In the early centuries of the Church it was the bishop who determined whether or not a certain candidate was a fit subject for ordination.[57] This power, however, was gradually limited so that Pope Alexander III decreed that if the crime was occult the bishop could merely exhort or persuade the guilty one not to ascend to higher orders, but if the latter insisted upon receiving them, then he could not be prohibited from doing so.[58] Pope Gregory IX, in 1229, legislated in similar fashion. He made only one exception, and that was the crime of homicide, which of itself begot an irregularity; as for the rest, whether it was adultery, perjury or any other crime that could not be proved in a trial, they could not be used by a bishop as the reason for hindering the exercise of orders already received or for barring anyone from advancing to higher orders.[59] Once an order was received, the bishop was powerless to prohibit its exercise, although he was aware of the fact that a certain occult crime was committed. Only when guilt could be determined in a formal trial could the

---

cum praepositorum scandalo, graduum altiorum appetere dignitatem; ei, cui ascensus ad sacros ordines a suo praelato, ex quacumque causa, etiam ob occultum crimen, quomodolibet, etiam extrajudicialiter, fuerit interdictus; aut qui a suis ordinibus seu gradibus vel dignitatibus ecclesiasticis fuerit suspensus; nulla contra ipsius praelati voluntatem concessa licentia de se promoveri faciendo; aut ad priores ordines, gradus, dignitates sive honores, restitutio suffragetur."

[57] Pallotini, *Pugna Juris Pontificii Statuentis Suspensiones extra-judicialiter seu ex Informata Conscientia, et Imperii easdem obrogare* Molientis (Viennae, 1863), pp. 74-76.

[58] C. 4, X, *de temporibus ordinationum,* I, 11: "Ex tenore tuarum litterarum accepimus, quod N. clericus adeo deliquit, quod, si peccatum eius esset publicum, degraderetur ab ordine, quem suscepit, et amplius non posset ad superiores ordines promoveri. Verum, quoniam peccatum ipsius fore occultum et privatum dixisti, fraternitati tuae per apostolica scripta mandamus, quatenus poenitentiam ei condignam imponas, et ei suadeas, ut parte poenitentiae peracta ordine suscepto utatur, quo cententus existens ad superiores ordines amplius non ascendat. Verum tamen, quia peccatum occultum est, si promoveri voluerit, eum non potes nec debes aliqua ratione prohibere."

[59] C. 17, X, *de temporibus ordinationum,* I, 11.

bishop take definite action. From such a sentence appeal could be made to a higher authority.

The Council of Trent had a certain precedent in the privilege that had been extended by Pope Lucius III (1181-1185) to the superiors of religious orders.[60] To them this pope had given the right to prohibit their subjects from advancing to higher orders when they knew them guilty even of secret crimes. The Council, however, went further than this when it gave to ordinaries the power to prohibit even the use of orders, degrees or dignities already received. This procedure was permitted even when accomplished *extrajudicialiter.* When such a penalty had been imposed, recourse to the Holy See alone could be had.

Hereafter one finds no further development in the penal powers possessed and exercised by the bishop as ordinary of the diocese. He it was who served as an instrument in carrying on the commission first entrusted to the apostles by Christ, to teach all nations, and in carrying out that office was acknowledged as possessing all requisite coercive power to preserve order, to punish and to reform recalcitrant members, and to safeguard the precepts of God as preached and propagated by Christ Himself.

---

[60] C. 5, X, *de temporibus ordinationum,* I, 11.

CHAPTER V

Participation in the Episcopal Jurisdiction in the Church

ARTICLE I. THE ARCHDEACON

Just when the office of the archdeacon came into being is difficult to say, but it can easily be surmised that the ready occasion for its institution arose after the Church was granted freedom by the Emperor Constantine in 313. The liturgy began to develop more rapidly; the faithful became more numerous, and accordingly the work of the bishop became more varied and manifold. The archdeacon's coercive power in the Church was a matter of gradual development. When the office first came into existence,[1] his work was primarily one of administration, for he was charged with the care of the poor and acted as supervisor of the other deacons. To him was entrusted the task of serving as overseer of the junior clergy, taking care of the proper fulfillment of the duties entrusted to them as well as of their training. The Council of Chalcedon (451)[2] gave him the right to remove a deacon who had become guilty of crime, or at least to deprive him temporarily of communion with the body of the faithful; if one of the lower clergy needed correction, he could even resort to corporal punishment. Later he is entrusted with the visitation and supervision of the clergy of the diocese. The Council of Auxerre (578) decreed that if a priest, deacon or subdeacon had begotten children or had committed adultery after being elevated to that order, he was to be deposed.[3] The commission of this act was to be made known to the bishop or archbishop by the archpriest. Thus

---

[1] Cf. Sozomen, *Ecclesiastical History* (Nicene and Post-Nicene Fathers, 2 series, New York, 1906), IV, 28; VI, 30; VIII, 9; Theodoretus, *Ecclesiastical History* (Nicene and Post-Nicene Fathers, 2 series, New York, 1906), I, 25.

[2] C. 10—Harduin, II, 610.

[3] C. 20—Harduin, III, 445.

gradually evolved the archdeacon's right and power to impose coercive measures. The Council of Agde (506) declared that if any cleric is overly concerned about the care of his hair in a way that is unbefitting his state, the archdeacon may take measures to stop the abuse, even cutting his hair.[4]

There is not to be found any definite statement as to the penal powers that the archdeacon could exercise without the approval of the bishop. He acted as the head of the canons gathered about the bishop, and to him was entrusted their care and discipline, receiving, in virtue of the office held, the power to inflict public penances, fasts, corporal punishment and even excommunication.[5] In the regulations promulgated by St. Chrodegang, Bishop of Metz (742-766), there is found the order that on all Sundays and on the feast days of the greater saints clerics were to assemble for the office of the day; if anyone failed to be present, it was the duty of the archdeacon to correct him, to impose corporal punishment or even to refuse him communion with the others.[6]

More and more was the archdeacon's power exercised in the work which he was sharing to a certain extent with the bishop, namely, that of making visitations of the diocese. He preceded the bishop, and, in order to relieve his superior of the minor affairs, would summon before himself those who were guilty of a crime or misconduct and decide their cases as he deemed just, inflicting whatever measures were necessary.[7]

The practice of dividing a diocese into various sections with each section entrusted to an archdeacon gradually became necessary because of both the constantly increasing diocesan activities, and the growing interests of the bishops in the affairs of their respective nations. Under these conditions the bishops gradually withdrew themselves, as it were, from the immediate care of the episcopal activities, from certain phases of it especially.

---

[4] C. 20—Harduin, II, 1000; cf. also, IV Council of Orleans (541), c. 26—Harduin, II, 1439; Council of Chalon-sur-Saône (650), c. 14—Harduin, III, 950.

[5] Council of Aix-la-Chapelle (816), c. 134—Mansi, XIV, 238.

[6] *Regula Chrodegangi*, c. 8—Mansi, XIV, 318.

[7] *Capitulum Walteri Aurelianensis episcopi* (871)—Mansi, XV, 507; Council of Rouen (878), c. 16—Harduin, VI, 208.

Naturally the archdeacon's influence became pronounced, for he was losing much of his former dependence on the bishop.

Consequently during the course of the twelfth century the archdeacon is found exercising episcopal jurisdiction, to a certain extent, as something that by right pertained to his office. Only for certain specified acts did he need episcopal approval.[8] These enactments, in the light of historical evidence, actually reveal that the archdeacon did not always conduct the affairs of his office within the properly indicated limits of his power.

The thirteenth century marked the zenith of the archdeacon's power. Pope Innocent III referred to him as *iudex ordinarius,* mentioning him together with the bishop as having such power.[9] The Council of Valence (1258) wrote to the "Bishop or the ordinary, otherwise known as the archdeacon,"[10] while the Council of Noyon (1280) spoke in like manner when it referred to the archdeacon or any other official having ordinary jurisdiction.[11] This view, that the archdeacon was an ordinary and had ordinary jurisdiction, was approved and followed by many of the Decretalists and commentators.[12] Nevertheless Barbosa maintained that the jurisdiction enjoyed by the archdeacon was not the same as

---

[8] C. 5, X, *de officio archidiaconi,* I, 23: "Archidiaconis non videtur de Ecclesiastica institutione licere (nisi autoritas Episcoporum accesserit) in aliquos sententiam promulgare." Cf. also, c. 7, § 6, X, *de officio archidiaconi,* I, 23; c. 3, X, *de poenis,* V, 37.

[9] "Inhibemus ne dioecesanus episcopus vel archidiaconus loci seu quilibet alius ordinarius iudex . . . sententiam promulgare praesumat." *Regesta,* lib. XIV, *ep. 45, Abbatissae Auregniacensi—MPL,* CCXVI, 413; cf. also, c. 10, X, *de officio archidiaconi,* I, 23.

[10] Harduin, VII, 1983.

[11] C. 1—Mansi, XXIV, 819.

[12] Hostiensis, *Summa Aurea* (Venetiis, 1570), Lib. I, *de officio archidiaconi,* n. 4; Panormitanus, Abbas (Nicolaus de Tudeschis), *Commentaria in Quinque Libros Decretalium* (Venetiis, 1588), Lib. I, *de officio archidiaconi,* cap. I, n. 2; Barbosa, *Collectanea Doctorum tam Veterum quam Recentiorum in Ius Pontificium Universum* (Lugduni, 1716), Tom. I, Tit. XXIII, n. 5; Thomassinus, Pars I, lib. II, cap. XIX, n. 12; Pirhing, *Jus Canonicum Nova Methodo Explicatum* (Dilingae, 1675), Lib. I, Tit. XXIII, n. 5; Reiffenstuel, Lib. I, Tit. XXIII, n. 6; Schmalzgrueber, *Ius Ecclesisiasticum Universum* (5 vols. in 12, Romae, 1843-1845), Tom. I, Pars IV, Tit. XXIII, n. 7.

that possessed by the bishop, but was inferior to it,[13] while Reiffenstuel held that the jurisdiction was distinct from that of the bishop; it was inferior and subordinate to that of the bishop.[14]

It was generally admitted that he was able to impose a mild penalty or to suspend a cleric for a short time. Those cases, however, which demanded as their punishment deposition, perpetual suspension or a prolonged suspension, could not be judged or decided by him alone.[15] Hostiensis maintained that due to custom the archdeacon was able to inflict excommunications, although he could not anathematize any person, for one inferior to the bishop was unable to excommunicate with the solemnity required.[16]

That this view is probably correct seems to be supported by the decrees of the councils which were promulgated as the office of the archdeacon began to lose its power, for many councils forbade this official to impose an excommunication, leading to the conclusion that such was hitherto done. Because of this jurisdiction that had gradually come to the archdeacon, he at times became, as it were, a threat to the authority possessed by the bishop.[17]

Within his territory it was the duty of the archdeacon to supervise and to care for the ecclesiastical affairs, exercising a careful surveillance over the behaviour and conduct of the ecclesiastics and seeing to it that the obligations of their office were observed. One Council in Germany (1225) made a special and determined effort to uproot an evil that had been existing among the clergy, the practice of keeping mistresses. The task of taking proper steps against this evil was assigned to the archdeacon. If he in any way neglected his duty or condoned the excesses then taking place, he was to be suspended from his office, and

---

[13] *Op. cit.*, Tom. I, Tit. XXIII, n. 4.

[14] Lib. I, Tit. XXIII, n. 6; cf. Hostiensis, *op. cit.*, Lib. I, *de officio archidiaconi*, n. 4.

[15] Barbosa, *Collectanea,* Tom. I, Tit. XXIII, nn. 2, 4; Panormitanus, Lib. I, *de officio archidiaconi*, cap. VII, n. 1; Engel, *Collegium Universi Iuris Canonici* (Venetiis, 1760), Lib. I, Tit. XXIII, n. 2.

[16] *Summa Aurea*, Lib. I, *de officio archidiaconi*, nn. 4, 5.

[17] C. 10, X, *de officio archidiaconi*, I, 23; c. 3, X, *de poenis*, V, 37.

if he nevertheless continued to abide in his suspension, he was then to be deprived of all his ecclesiastical dignities by the bishop.[18]

In the Gregorian Decretals it is stated that it was the archdeacon's duty to see to the proper conduct of the clergy and to give such precepts as were in harmony with the various ecclesiastical orders received. If the bishop was unable to conduct the visitation personally, then the archdeacon was to undertake it, and if anyone needed correction, he was to proceed with the proper corrective measures.[19]

The thirteenth century marked the zenith of the development of the powers enjoyed by the archdeacon. Because of other activities, however, the archdeacons gradually began to neglect their territories, or at least did not attend personally to the duties incumbent upon them in virtue of their office, appointing assistants under the title of *officiales*[20] or *vicarii*.[21] Accordingly, legislation soon followed which deprived the archdeacon of the power of appointing assistants,[22] while the bishops appointed other assistants as immediate and personal representatives.[23]

Though the archdeacon's office was gradually deprived of many powers that it had in regard to penal matters, especially such as the disciplinary powers over the clergy, it was not at once discontinued. It was only gradually that power upon power was withdrawn until the time of the Council of Trent. This Council no longer permitted the undertaking of the diocesan visitation as an official duty.[24] No longer could he proceed against clerics,

---

[18] C. 3—Mansi, XXIII, 3; cf. also the Council of Rouen (1231), c. 10—Harduin, VII, 1086.

[19] C. 1, X, *de officio archidiaconi*, I, 23; Ferraris, *Prompta Bibliotheca*, "Archidiaconus," n. 10.

[20] C. 3, X, *de novi operis nunciatione*, V, 32; Council of Oxford (1222), c. 27—Mansi, XXIII, 1159; *Constitutiones synodales Episcopi anonymi* (c. 1237)—Mansi, XXIII, 474; Synod of Exeter (1238), c. 42—Mansi, XXIV, 824.

[21] Council of Cognac (1238), c. 4—Mansi, XXIII, 488.

[22] Council of Chateau Gontier (1231), c. 13—Mansi, XXIII, 236; Council of Tours (1239), c. 8—Mansi, XXIV, 627.

[23] C. 3, X, *de institutionibus*, III, 7; Council of Rouen (1190), c. 22—Harduin, VII, 1907.

[24] Sess. XXIV, *de ref.*, c. 3.

not even against those who lived in concubinage contrary to the laws of the Church.[25] Finally, the power to inflict excommunications, a power which he had enjoyed to a certain extent, was taken from him.[26]

Thus the archdeacon, who in the beginning was considered the first assistant of the bishop, and who later became an almost independent power in his own territory, gradually lost his importance, and became in ecclesiastical affairs an almost meaningless functionary.

ARTICLE II. THE VICAR-GENERAL

It is in the *Liber Sextus* of the *Corpus Iuris Canonici* that the term *officialis* is found for the first time, and a study of the history of the term and office will show that it was often used to designate not only the office of the *officialis* as he is known today[27] but also that of the vicar-general.[28] For many centuries these two offices were not differentiated except in name;[29] the laws that were promulgated made no distinction, sometimes speaking of the *vicarius,* sometimes of the *officialis.* Even in the eighteenth century Pope Benedict XIV tells us that there was a distinction made in certain places only, none, however, was made in Italy.[30]

Just when these offices came into being is difficult to determine precisely. Thomassinus would look back to the third or fourth centuries for their origin.[31] It seems more correct, however, to hold that they arose during the thirteenth century, when the bishops found it necessary to associate with themselves assistants

---

[25] Sess. XIV, *de ref.*, c. 14.

[26] Sess. XIV, *de ref.*, c. 3.

[27] Tobin, *De Officiali Curiae Diocesanae* (Romae: Apud Aedes Pontificae Universitatis Gregorianae, 1936), p. 24.

[28] Campagna, *Il Vicario Generale del Vescovo* (Catholic University of America, Canon Law Studies, n. 66, Washington, D. C.: The Catholic University of America, 1931), p. 30; Fournier, *Les Origines du Vicaire General* (Paris, 1922), p. 10.

[29] Barbosa, *De Officio et Potestate Episcopi* (Lugduni, 1656), Pars III, n. 53.

[30] *De Synodo Dioecesana,* Lib. III, cap. 3, n. 2.

[31] Pars I, Lib. II, Cap. VII.

who would relieve them of some of the tasks incumbent upon them.[32] Thomassinus himself points out that neither in the Decree of Gratian nor in the Decretals of Gregory IX is any trace of these offices found.[33]

As the office of the vicar-general developed and continued after the thirteenth century, he was the representative of the bishop, assisting him in the exercise of his jurisdiction; whatever powers he possessed, he exercised in the place and in the name of the bishop. His powers dealt with the administration of spiritual matters, being referred to as the *vicarius generalis episcopi*[34] or *vicarius in spiritualibus generalis.*[35] The presence in a diocese of an *officialis,* appointed primarily to administer temporal and civil affairs, shows that the vicar-general's work was chiefly the care of spiritualities. Still, if conditions required, both offices could be united in one person.[36]

Although the vicar-general was the bishop's assistant and with him formed, as it were, one person in the administration of his office, positive law forbade the exercise of jurisdiction in certain instances, demanding that a special mandate of the bishop be given. Thus the vicar-general could not exercise criminal and coercive powers; he was not permitted to inflict certain censures and penalties, such as suspensions[37] and excommunications,[38] for excesses committed by his subjects.[39]

The vicar-general was further required to have a special mandate to grant dispensations from irregularities and censures imposed for occult crimes, yet he was not to be delegated in cases which involved the crime of heresy, for this was withheld by

---

[32] Wernz, *Ius Decretalium* (6 vols., Romae, 1906-1913), II, 635.

[33] Pars I, Lib. II, Cap. VIII, n. 1.

[34] C. 3, *de officio vicarii,* I, 13, in VI°.

[35] C. 3, *de temporibus ordinationum,* I, 9, in VI°.

[36] Barbosa, *De Officio et Potestate Episcopi,* Pars III, All. 54, n. 57; Engel, *Collegium Universi Juris Canonici,* I, 28, n. 3; Bouix, *Tractatus de Judiciis Ecclesiasticis* (2 vols., Parisiis, 1855), I, 355.

[37] Kober, *Die Suspension,* p. 41.

[38] Kober, *Der Kirchenbann,* p. 74.

[39] C. 2, *de officio vicarii,* I, 13, in VI°; Barbosa, *Collectanea,* Tom. IV, Lib. I, Tit. IV, cap. III, n. 4; Bouix, *Tractatus de Judiciis,* I, 415, 435.

express mention and decree of the Council of Trent.[40] In view of the fact that the vicar-general was forbidden the exercise of penal powers without special mandate, he was prohibited from demanding the *purgatio canonica,*[41] from imposing confiscation as a punishment on a cleric,[42] and finally from granting absolution for excommunications or other censures when these were *latae sententiae.*[43]

The vicar-general, therefore, did not possess jurisdiction in criminal and penal affairs in view of his office; it is true, he constituted "one person" with the bishop in the administration of his office in so far as no appeal could be made from one to the other, still he did require a mandate from the bishop to exercise jurisdiction in criminal matters.

ARTICLE III. THE OFFICIALIS

Van Espen thinks that the office of the *officialis,* in its present conception as a judge, was established as early as the twelfth century, for he says that already at that time *officiales* were functioning in Gaul.[44] With him P. Fournier fully agrees, for he also holds that the office was in existence in Gaul in the second half of the twelfth century.[45] This new official was appointed to assist the bishop in judging in ecclesiastical matters, most especially in criminal cases involving the clergy. These cases gradually had become reserved to the ecclesiastical court through the legislation of Charlemagne,[46] King Henry I of Germany (919-936)[47] and Pope Lucius III (1181-1185).[48]

---

[40] Sess. XXIV, *de ref.*, c. 6.

[41] A canonical method of establishing innocence, in which the accused declared his innocence under oath.

[42] Barbosa, *De Officio et Potestate Episcopi,* Pars III, Alleg. 54, n. 119; Ferraris, *Prompta Bibliotheca,* "Vicarius Generalis," Art. II, n. 79.

[43] Barbosa, *op. cit.,* Pars III, Alleg. 54, n. 96; Ferraris, *ibid.*, n. 63.

[44] *Ius Ecclesiasticum Universum,* Vol. II, Pars III, Tit. V, cap. 1.

[45] P. Fournier, *Les Officialites au Moyen Age* (Paris, 1880), p. 3.

[46] Caroli Magni, Ludovici et Lotharii Capitularia ab Ansagiso Abbate Fontanellensi Collecta—*Capitula ecclesiastica Caroli Magni,* cap. 38—*MPL,* XCVII, 513.

[47] *Monumenta Germaniae Historica, Leges,* Tom. II, p. 17.

[48] C. 8, X, *de iudiciis,* II, 1.

Since the *officialis* was the assistant in judicial matters, he exercised certain and definite powers, but the power to inflict penalties was given him, not in virtue of his appointment, but only in view of a special mandate.[49] Pirhing (1606-1679) stated that among the cases that demand a special commission, and which therefore are not included in the office as generally granted, are those dealing with criminal matters.[50] Other authors held the same opinion, namely, that without such a special mandate the *officialis* could not proceed in criminal cases.[51] Sanchez (1550-1610) wrote that, although the *officialis* is said to have jurisdiction in civil affairs, spiritual matters were not to be excluded with the exception of criminal affairs, for the *officialis* was not permitted to undertake these without a special commission.[52]

That the special mandate which the *officialis* needed could be readily granted to him may be seen from the decrees of certain councils and synods.[53] This was natural, for, as already pointed out, the multiplication of the duties of the bishop made it imperative at times for the bishop to relieve himself of some of the tasks by appointing others to act in his stead.

In the exercise of his office the *officialis* as judge was not a superior; accordingly he could not enact new laws or penalties, but simply was to apply the penalties already legitimately enacted. In only a very few instances did he possess the power and right to exercise, in a certain sense, any coercive powers in accordance with his own discretion.

The first of these instances was in regard to slanderous speech offered by a witness during a trial. This offense was always

---

[49] C. 2, *de officio vicarii,* I, 13, in VI°.

[50] Lib. I, tit. XXVIII, sect. II, n. 44.

[51] Barbosa, *De Officio et potestate episcopi,* Pars III, Alleg. LIV, n. 117; Reiffenstuel, Lib. I, tit. XXVIII, n. 80; Schmalzgrueber, Tom. I, Pars IV, tit. XXVIII, n. 23.

[52] *De Sancto Matrimonii Sacramento Disputationum Libri Sex* (Lugduni, 1669), Tom. I, Lib. III, disp. XXIX, n. 16.

[53] Synod of Clermont (1268), c. 10—Mansi, XXIII, 1211; Council of Bourges (1286), c. 35—Mansi, XXIV, 642; Council of Narbonne (1374), c. 6—Harduin, VIII, 1880; Council of Rouen (1445), c. 24—Harduin, X, 1298; Council of Avignon (1509), c. 22—Mansi, XXXII, 544.

considered most serious. The Council of Elvira (305)[54] had decreed that a calumniator was to be deprived of communion, and if such an accusation was made against a bishop, a priest or a deacon, he should be deprived of communion even at the hour of death. This law was later relaxed by the Council of Orleans (541) to the extent that communion could be restored in the hour of death.[55] Later Pope Gregory the Great, deciding in a case that involved a subdeacon who had spoken calumny, stated that such a one was to be deprived of any office or benefice which he held, and could even be condemned to flagellation and exile.[56] The infliction of such a penalty naturally depended to a great extent on the assistance of the secular power. Once this assistance was withdrawn, one thus found guilty was subject to the punishments within the scope of the Church's power, namely, ecclesiastical censures.[57]

In cases such as this it was the judge who had to decide not only whether calumny was actually present, but also whether there were present any excusing causes which might mitigate the rigor of the penalties attached to the offense of calumny. The Council of Trent in no way changed these measures, although it did advise that censures should be used as a last resort only.[58] Reiffenstuel tells us that although the law permitting exile and flagellation continued, a long established custom had withheld such punishment from being inflicted.[59] It was for the judge, then, to decide the punishment that would be imposed.

A second instance in which the judge could act within certain limits upon his own discretion was in regard to the summoning of witnesses. In 1170 Pope Alexander III wrote that a witness when known to be such, was to be cited by the judge to appear in court to offer his testimony. If it happened that such a witness, after being properly cited, refused to appear, the judge was to

---

[54] C. 75—Harduin, I, 256.
[55] C. 29—Harduin, II, 1439.
[56] C. 1, X, *de calumniatoribus*, V, 2.
[57] C. 2, X, *de calumniatoribus*, V, 2.
[58] Sess. XXV, *de ref.*, c. 3.
[59] Lib. V, Tit. II, n. 10.

inquire into the reasons for the refusal, and, if he felt justified, might even force the witness to testify.[60] For the interpretation of the laws pertaining to this question, it is necessary to consult the commentators.[61] A second citation with the threat of punishment had to intervene before any ecclesiastical penalties could be inflicted. Pirhing states that if a witness, after being warned, refused to testify, he was presumed to be withholding the truth for some questionable motive and therefore could be compelled by the judge to testify.[62] There were exceptions, however, in regard to the need of a warning. If the testimony was such that it was immediately necessary, the judge could threaten punishment immediately.[63] This punishment could consist of such penalties as excommunication or interdict. In the case of a cleric the judge could force him under pain of suspension; but if this penal measure proved vain as a remedy, then the judge could resort to the infliction of excommunication and other similarly severe penalties.[64] For one who impeded a witness in such a way as to make it impossible for him to appear, the judge could proceed to an excommunication. Farinacius states that no explicit law existed in regard to this latter practice, but that the procedure was one commonly followed.[65]

According to the laws of Alexander III (1151-1189) and his successors, the judge was not to force a witness to testify in criminal matters under ordinary circumstances. Thus Pope Honorius III (1216-1227), when permitting the compelling of a witness, made an explicit exception in regard to criminal cases.[66] Exception was made, however, when the testimony could not otherwise be had or when a witness was maliciously impeded from testifying.

---

[60] Cc. 1, 3, 6, 9, X, *de testibus cogendis,* II, 21.

[61] Gonzalez-Tellez, *Commentaria,* Lib. II, Tit. XXI, cap. 1, n. 3; Pirhing, *Jus Canonicum,* Lib. II, tit. XXI, n. 3; Reiffenstuel, Lib. II, tit. XXI, sec. I, n. 2; Panormitanus, Lib. II, tit. XXI, cap. I.

[62] *Jus Canonicum,* Lib. II, tit. XXI, n. 4.

[63] C. 1, X, *de testibus cogendis,* II, 21.

[64] C. 2, X, *de testibus cogendis,* II, 21.

[65] *Tractatus de Testibus* (Venetiis, 1609), q. 78, n. 138.

[66] C. 10, X, *de testibus cogendis,* II, 21.

In the application of these measures the judge was to use his discretion. In this respect the Council of Trent made no changes. In criminal cases the judge could use his discretion to threaten and ultimately to inflict excommunication as a last resort, but only after having employed at least a twofold fruitless warning.[67]

Thus the law remained; later councils and practice in ecclesiastical courts have never altered this legislation.

ARTICLE IV. THE PASTOR

All pastors enjoy the *potestas ordinis* which flows from their reception of the Sacrament of Holy Orders, and the *potestas magisterii,* which is derived from their priesthood. It has always been conceded that the pastor possesses jurisdiction in the internal forum; any jurisdiction in the external forum that has been attributed to him has to do with the infliction of censures and penalties, a contention substantiated, in a certain sense, by instances in history. Of these the outstanding instance is the one found in the Decretals in which Pope Alexander III decreed that an excommunication which had been imposed by a pastor on any of his subjects should be considered justified and was not to be removed by the bishop without the approval of the pastor.[68]

The same pope, Alexander III, in about the year 1170, approved the action of the Archbishop of Rheims who had removed an excommunication inflicted by a priest who had seemingly acted in haste.[69]

These are not the only instances in which pastors exercised

---

[67] Sess. XXV, *de ref.*, c. 3.

[68] "Quum ab ecclesiarum praelatis ecclesiastica sententia in malefactores aliquos promulgatur, rata debet et firma consistere, et usque ad condignam satisfactionem inviolabiliter observari. Quapropter discretioni vestrae per apostolica scripta mandamus, quatenus, si quando dilectus filius noster Lan., . . . in clericos vel laicos parochianos suos interdicti vel excommunicationis sententiam rationabiliter tulerit, ipsam facias inviolabiliter observari, et eam sine congrua satisfactione et absque eiusdem plebani conscientia non relaxes."—C. 3, X, *de officio iudicis ordinarii,* I, 31.

[69] *Epistola LI* (ad Petrum Abbatem S. Remigii)—Mansi, XXI, 956.

this power, for there exists legislation of the twelfth and thirteenth centuries concerning the infliction of penalties by pastors.[70] These instances, however, do not necessarily imply that the power here spoken of was considered a *ius ordinarium,* a right that was possessed and exercised in virtue of the office held. Excommunications, at times, were inflicted, not in virtue of a personal right, but as acts of usurped authority. Thus the Council of Tours (1239) decreed that rectors of parochial churches could not excommunicate in virtue of any authority they possessed or in view of the office they exercised.[71]

The one citation of the general law that seemingly disproves this explanation is that of Pope Alexander III mentioned above, but authors agree that this must be accepted as an exception to the rule, considering it a right based upon a special title or upon prescription.

St. Thomas Aquinas in considering the power of pastors to impose excommunications said that although the pastor, as a priest, possesses the power of binding and loosing, he can exercise that power in the internal forum only. Therefore, he concluded, only bishops and major superiors (*praelati*), according to the more common opinion, can excommunicate, but parish priests cannot.[72]

Commenting on the canon cited from the Decretals, canonists in general have reached the same conclusion. Gonzalez-Tellez in his commentary states that Joannes Andreas and Hostiensis contended that the pastor possesses this power. The author does not agree with them, however, for he holds that excommunication is a censure that is proper to the ecclesiastical forum, and the pastor as such cannot act as a *iudex ordinarius.* He does not deny, however, that this power could be given him by special delegation or as a privilege.[73] With him Barbosa[74] and Fag-

---

[70] *Communia Praecepta* (Odo, Episcopus Parisii), nn. 45, 58—Mansi, XXII, 683; Synod of Nismes (1284)—Mansi, XXIV, 552.

[71] C. 6—Mansi, XXIII, 499.

[72] *Commentaria in Quatuor Libros Sententiarum Petri Lombardi,* Lib. V, cap. 4, n. 2.

[73] *Commentaria,* Lib. I, tit. XXXI, cap. III, n. 2.

[74] *Collectanea,* Lib. I, tit. XXXI, cap. 3.

nanus[75] agree, basing the right which was exercised by the priest as mentioned in the Decretals not on a right inherent in the office he held, but on privilege or prescription.

In May, 1654, the Congregation for the Propagation of the Faith was asked by missionaries in India if it was permissible to one in the exercise of parochial affairs to impose censures for the punishment and correction of delinquents. The answer given was in the negative, without any distinction or exception.[76]

The contention that a pastor as such could exercise penal powers in virtue of his pastoral office has had little credence or sympathy throughout the centuries. One may, therefore, safely accept the opinion of those authors who hold that any penal power that was exercised by pastors in the past was based upon delegation or privilege, and was never generally considered as something inherent in the pastoral office itself.

---

[75] *Commentaria in Quinque Libros Decretalium* (Venetiis, 1696), Lib. I, tit, XXXI, cap. 3, n. 2.

[76] *Collectanea S. Cong. de Prop. Fide,* I, 120; cf. *Fontes,* n. 4460.

PART TWO

Canonical Commentary

CHAPTER VI

Ecclesiastical Superiors Possessing Coercive Powers

Canon 2220

§ 1: Qui pollent potestate leges ferendi vel praecepta imponendi, possunt quoque legi vel praecepto poenas adnectere; qui iudiciali tantum, possunt solummodo poenas, legitime statutas, ad normam iuris applicare.

§ 2: Vicarius Generalis sine mandato speciali non habet potestatem infligendi poenas.

Ecclesiastical jurisdiction may be defined as a public power, either granted by God or bestowed by the Church, of ruling over baptized subjects with a view to securing their eternal salvation.[1] By reason of the forum in which it is exercised, the power of jurisdiction is divided into jurisdiction of the internal forum and jurisdiction of the external forum.[2] Jurisdiction of the external forum is concerned directly and primarily with the Church as a visible society, promoting its common good and directing the actions of the faithful. The infliction of coercive measures is an act of jurisdiction pertaining to the external forum, and therefore

---

[1] Maroto, *Institutiones Iuris Canonici ad Normam Novi Codicis* (2 vols., Madrid, 1919), I, n. 573; Noldin-Schmitt, *Summa Theologiae Moralis* (26. ed., 3 vols., Oeniponte, 1939), I, n. 129; Vermeersch-Creusen, *Epitome Iuris Canonici* (3 vols., Vol. I, 6 ed., Vols. II and III, 5 ed., Mechliniae-Romae: H. Dessain, 1934-1937), I, n. 233; Wernz-Vidal, *Ius Canonicum ad Codicis Normam Exactum* (7 tom. in 8 vols., Romae: Apud Aedes Universitatis Gregorianae, 1929-1938), II, n. 48.

[2] Canon 196.

only those who enjoy the use of jurisdiction in the external forum are competent to inflict such measures.[3] Hence all others who either totally lack the power of jurisdiction, as the laity, or those who possess this power only in the internal forum or in an administrative capacity, as the pastor, are incompetent to inflict censures.[4]

Jurisdiction is further divided into ordinary and delegated jurisdiction. Ordinary jurisdiction is that which is automatically attached to an office,[5] so that one who legitimately acquires an office also acquires the jurisdiction attached to that office. Delegated jurisdiction is not attached to an office *ipso facto*, but is obtained through commission by a competent superior to a particular person.[6]

By divine institution the hierarchy of jurisdiction consists of the Supreme Pontificate and the subordinate episcopate.[7] Hence it is only the Pope, as the successor of Saint Peter,[8] and the bishops, as successors of the Apostles,[9] who exercise jurisdiction as established by divine right. All others who exercise jurisdiction in the external forum have been granted such power by purely ecclesiastical law.[10]

With these preliminary distinctions in mind, one may now proceed to a more detailed and specific consideration of those offices, whether of divine or ecclesiastical institution, whose incumbents possess jurisdiction in the external forum, and who, because of their possession of this power, are competent to legislate and to add determinate sanctions to the laws enacted.

---

[3] Cappello, *Tractatus Canonico-Moralis de Censuris juxta Codicem Iuris Canonici* (3. ed., Taurinorum Augustae: Marietti, 1933), p. 11, n. 10; Lega, *De Delictis et Poenis* (Romae, 1910), p. 149, n. 103.

[4] Cappello, *De Censuris*, n. 10; Cipollini, A., *De Censuris Latae Sententiae iuxta Codicem Iuris Canonici* (Taurini, 1925), n. 15, 11o.

[5] Canon 197, § 1.

[6] Canon 197, § 1.

[7] Canon 108, § 3.

[8] Conc. Vat., Sess. IV, cap. 1, 2, 3—*Coll. Lac.*, VII, 269.

[9] Conc. Trid., Sess. XXIII, cap. 4.

[10] Wernz-Vidal, *Ius Canonicum*, II, n. 49.

ARTICLE I. SUPREME JURISDICTION IN THE CHURCH

A. The Pope

The Council of the Vatican declared anathema anyone who denies that the Roman Pontiff is the successor of St. Peter, and as such holds the primacy over the universal Church by divine right.[11] The same penalty was threatened upon those who deny that the Pontiff possesses disciplinary and coercive powers over the entire Church, a power that is supreme, ordinary and immediate, affecting not only individuals as such but the Church as a whole.[12]

The power of jurisdiction possessed by the pope is supreme, there being no human superior or equal. This extension of power is consequent upon the very constitution of the Church, which is of purely monarchical formation,[13] and is equal to every social demand made upon it.[14] Accordingly there are no limits placed upon his powers, save only those of the divine law, whether natural or positive, contrary to which he may not act and from which he may not dispense.[15] In the valid exercise of his power he is limited only by this superior law and the religious and spiritual needs of the Church over which he reigns, while for the licit exercise thereof he must be directed by prudence and by the obligation to work for the Church's advancement and the removal of all that is deleterious.[16]

It further follows that the jurisdiction possessed by the Supreme Pontiff is truly episcopal[17] not only in that he has the right to teach the universal Church, but in that he also has the right to impose laws and precepts which beget moral and juridic obliga-

---

[11] Sess. IV, canon 2—*Coll. Lac.*, VII, 273.

[12] Sess. IV, can. 3—*Coll. Lac.*, VII, 273.

[13] Toso, *Ad Codicem Iuris Canonici Commentaria Minora* (5 vols., Romae: Marietti, 1920-1934), Lib. II, Tom. II, p. 10.

[14] Ryan, *Principles of Episcopal Jurisdiction* (The Catholic University of America, Canon Law Studies, n. 120, Washington, D. C.: The Catholic University of America, 1939), p. 65.

[15] Chelodi, *Ius de Personis* (2. ed., Tridenti, 1921), n. 152; Toso, *Commentaria Minora*, Lib. II, Tom. II, p. 10.

[16] Chelodi, *Ius de Personis*, n. 152.

[17] Canon 218, § 2.

tions of such force that no human agency can resist them with impunity.[18] His jurisdiction is ordinary, enabling him to carry out his universal episcopal prerogatives, not merely as one substituting for a negligent bishop in his diocese, but as one having the right to act immediately and directly in view of the office which he holds, depending on no intermediary by whose delegation he may act.[19] To him the entire universe is one vast diocese in which he may exercise his primatial powers independent of human authority, and dependent upon God alone.[20] All are his subjects, whether they be superiors set over determined dioceses or territories, or whether they be the individual members of the laity; all are under his legal dominion, whether they be considered as assembled in council or whether they be regarded simply as individuals.[21]

Enjoying this primacy over the Church by divine institution, the pope therefore enjoys all the rights and prerogatives necessary for the proper fulfillment and exercise of his jurisdiction. Accordingly, he possesses not merely the plenitude of the priesthood, but the plenitude of jurisdiction—the power to legislate[22] and the power to fortify his laws and precepts with fitting sanctions.[23]

Because of the essentially universal character of the Church, there must exist matters for which the ordinary power of the residential bishop is inadequate, due to the fact that the bishop's power is diocesan while the matters considered are of a universal nature. Such matters are called the essential major causes (*causae maiores essentiales*), including all those which demand an exercise of papal infallibility as well as those purely disciplinary laws

---

[18] Coronata, *Institutiones Iuris Canonici* (5 vols., Taurini: Marietti, Vols. I, II, 2. ed., 1939; Vol. III, 1933; Vol. IV, 1935; Vol. V, 1936), I, n. 309; Toso, *Commentaria Minora*, Lib. II, Tom. II, p. 11; Wernz, *Ius Decretalium* (6 vols., Romae, 1906-1913), II, 592, I.

[19] Cavigioli, *De Censuris Latae Sententiae* (Torino, 1919), n. 7.

[20] Coronata, *Institutiones*, I, n. 309.

[21] Coronata, *Institutiones*, I, n. 309; Eichmann, *Lehrbuch des Kirchenrechts auf Grund des Codex Iuris Canonici* (2. ed., Paderborn: Schoeningh, 1926), pp. 144-145; Wernz, *Ius Decretalium*, II, 586.

[22] Canon 218, § 1.

[23] Canon 2220, § 1.

which affect the universal Church.[24] Besides these essential causes, there are also those matters arising as a natural consequent of the territorial organization of the Church into dioceses, whether these matters arise from the relations of the dioceses among themselves, or from their individual relations with the Holy See. These, then, are the *causae maiores per se.*

More abundant than these foregoing major causes, however, are those which may be considered such *per accidens.* Although the matters included in this category are radically subject to the jurisdiction of the residential bishops, still they have been subjected by the enactments of positive ecclesiastical law to the higher authority of the supreme pontiff.[25] These may be withdrawn from the jurisdiction of the individual bishop, either for the promotion of the common good or because of their special gravity or the difficulty of their solution.[26] This intervention of the pope may be exercised by entirely withdrawing certain matters from the scope of the bishop's jurisdiction, by exempting certain persons, places, or things from the direct control of the ordinary, or by regulating the method of procedure in certain instances.[27]

Canon 2227, § 1, together with canon 1557, § 1, determines what these exemptions are when there is question of penal or coercive measures. Subject to the jurisdiction of the Roman Pontiff exclusively are those who hold the highest governmental rank in a nation, their sons and daughters, and those who have the immediate right of succession. Among these, then, would be included the king or queen of a nation and his or her consort, as also the president of a republic; in short, that one who is considered the ruler in any particular nation.[28] Another group enjoying this special privilege is that consisting of the Cardinals,

[24] Cavagnis, *Institutiones Iuris Publici,* II, 438; Chelodi, *Ius de Personis,* n. 152; Coronata, *Institutiones,* I, n. 309; Ryan, *Principles of Episcopal Jurisdiction,* p. 66; Toso, *Commentaria Minora,* Lib. II, Tom. II, p. 14.

[25] Cavagnis, *Institutiones Iuris Publici,* II, 439; Eichmann, *Kirchenrecht,* p. 145; Chelodi, *Ius de Personis,* n. 152; Ryan, *Principles of Episcopal Jurisdiction,* p. 91; Toso, *Commentaria Minora,* Lib. II, Tom. II, p. 14.

[26] Coronata, *Institutiones,* I, n. 309.

[27] Billot, *Tractatus de Ecclesia Christi* (5. ed., 2 vols., Romae: Apud Aedes Universitatis Gregorianae, 1927), I, 713.

[28] Coronata, *Institutiones,* IV, n. 1713.

Legates of the Holy See, and all bishops.[29] These exemptions, then, are, as it were, a certain restriction of the ordinary power of a residential bishop.

All major causes, therefore, whether they are such by their very nature or have been made such by positive legislation, are excluded from the jurisdictional competency of the individual bishop. Should the occasion arise, the bishop may ask that special provision be made for a particular territory in accordance with the peculiar local conditions then existent, but until such time as this special provision is forthcoming, the bishop must be guided by existing law.[30]

ARTICLE II. PARTICIPANTS IN THE SUPREME JURISDICTION IN THE CHURCH

A. *The Ecumenical Council*

Having universal power and the plenitude of jurisdiction, the Supreme Pontiff is under no necessity or obligation, whether of divine or ecclesiastical law, to convoke an ecumenical council, but may do so from motives of utility or because of a certain moral necessity to undertake more expeditiously the defining of dogmatic truths and the establishment of universal ecclesiastical discipline.[31] The basis of the power possessed by any ecumenical council is founded in the will of Christ Himself, and whatever power is predicated of the Supreme Pontiff considered independently is predicated also of an ecumenical council with the Pontiff at its head.[32]

The Roman Pontiff alone has the particular and exclusive right of convoking an ecumenical council, so that without this convocation there could be no real and lawful council.[33] The constitu-

---

[29] Canon 1557, § 1, nn. 2, 3.

[30] Ryan, *Principles of Episcopal Jurisdiction*, p. 94.

[31] Cf. Bouix, *Tractatus de Papa ubi et De Concilio Oecumenico* (3 vols., Parisiis, 1869-1870), III, 354; Palmieri, *Tractatus de Romano Pontifice* (2. ed., Prati, 1891), p. 695; Wernz-Vidal, *Ius Canonicum*, II, n. 459.

[32] Toso, *Commentaria Minora*, Lib. II, Tom. II, p. 23.

[33] Canon 222, § 1. Cf. Coronata, *Institutiones*, I, n. 320; Palmieri, *De Romano Pontifice*, p. 671; Phillips, *Kirchenrecht*, II, 237; Pesch, *Prae-*

tion of the Church, by divine institution, is monarchic, not democratic or aristocratic, and therefore all decrees of ecumenical councils lack binding force until such time as that they are confirmed by the Pontiff and promulgated in accordance with his discretion.[34] Although residential bishops have ordinary jurisdiction within their proper territory, they have not the power to legislate for the universal Church, whether they act individually or in council assembled, but can do so only when the council has been properly convoked by the Pontiff and its decrees approved by him.[35]

Properly constituted, an ecumenical council enjoys supreme and ordinary power.[36] Considered intensively, this power of the council is no greater than that of the Pope Himself, for to him was given supreme power by Christ Himself, other than which, with the pope at its head, the council does not enjoy.[37] An ecumenical council, therefore, is not incompetent to establish disciplinary and penal laws for the universal Church, nor is there excluded from its jurisdiction the direct and immediate infliction of ecclesiastical penalties on individual transgressors.[38]

B. The Cardinals

In pre-Code times there was some dispute as to whether a Cardinal possessed jurisdiction, and if so, how far it extended. Most authors agree that in view of the constitution *"Romanus Pontifex"* of Pope Innocent XII[39] all quasi-episcopal jurisdiction was withdrawn, and there remained only certain honorary

---

lectiones Dogmaticae (3. ed., Friburgi Brisgoviae. 1903), I, n. 448; Toso, *Commentaria Minora*, Lib. II, Tom. II, p. 18.

[34] Canon 227. Cf. Cavigioli, *De Censuris*, p. 16, n. 8; Eichmann, *Kirchenrecht*, p. 146; Wernz, *Ius Decretalium*, II, n. 850.

[35] Palmieri, *De Romano Pontifice*, p. 681.

[36] Canon 228, § 1. Pesch, *Praelectiones Dogmaticae*, I, n. 459; Wernz-Vidal, *Ius Canonicum*, II, n. 461.

[37] Bouix, *De Papa*, II, pp. 513, 687; Palmieri, *De Romano Pontifice*, p. 691.

[38] Bouix, *De papa*, III, 415; Wernz-Vidal, *Ius Canonicum*, II, n. 461.

[39] 17 sept. 1692—*Bullarium Romanum*, XX, n. 32, p. 461.

rights and a dominative power to be exercised over clerics immediately subject to them.[40]

The law as it exists today has reenacted the legislation of Innocent XII, for it declares that those Cardinals who do not rule over a bishopric enjoy in their churches all the rights and functions which a local ordinary enjoys, with the exception of presiding over canonical trials and of exercising acts of jurisdiction over the faithful, but including authority in matters pertaining to discipline in the correction of abuses and in the regulation of the service of their churches.[41] Hence a Cardinal, in view of this particular office, may use whatever measures he may deem necessary to restore discipline among those subject to him, but he may not proceed to the infliction of censures or vindictive penalties, for this power has not been granted him.[42]

Those Cardinals, however, who have been appointed to suburbicarian sees or to any other diocese throughout the world, do possess full jurisdiction even in penal matters. This power they possess, not because of their cardinalate, but because of their position as an ordinary of a diocese. Hence they enjoy all the rights and powers predicated of a residential bishop.[43]

C. *The Sacred Congregations*

Authors are unanimously agreed that the Sacred Congregations, when acting within the ambit of their competency[44] and issuing general decrees, have the power to inflict coercive measures, pro-

---

[40] Ballerini-Palmieri, *Opus Theologicum Morale* (7 vols., Prati, 1893), VII, n. 21; Cappello, *De Censuris*, n. 12; Santi, *Praelectiones Juris Canonici* (2. ed., 2 vols., Ratisbonae, Neo-Eboraci, Cincinnati, 1892), Lib. I, tit. 31, n. 34; Wernz, *Ius Decretalium*, II, n. 478.

[41] Canon 240, § 2.

[42] Cf. Cappello, *De Censuris*, n. 12; Cavigioli, *De Censuris*, n. 10; Chelodi, *Ius Poenale et Ordo Procedendi in Iudiciis Criminalibus iuxta Codicem Iuris Canonici* (Tridenti, 1925), n. 24, nota 1; *Ius de Personis*, n. 158 b; Eichmann, *Kirchenrecht*, p. 60.

[43] Canon 240, § 1. Cf. Cappello, *De Censuris*, n. 12; Chelodi, *Ius de Personis*, n. 158 b; Coronata, *Institutiones*, I, n. 325; Wernz, *Ius Decretalium*, II, n. 478; Wernz-Vidal, *Ius Canonicum*, II, n. 478.

[44] Canons 247-257.

vided the approbation of the Holy Father has been previously obtained.[45] This conclusion is drawn from the *Motu Proprio* of Benedict XV issued on the 15th of September, 1917.[46]

An example of the exercise of jurisdiction is the decree of the Congregation of the Consistory issued on December 30, 1918. The Congregation decreed a suspension *a divinis,* to which are *ipso facto* subject all priests who have rashly and contemptuously emigrated from Europe or the Mediterranean countries to America or the Philippines without having previously obtained the necessary permission in writing. In addition, the Congregation reserves to itself the right and power of granting absolution from this censure.[47]

Cappello, while agreeing that a general decree of the Congregations needs the approbation of the Supreme Pontiff, adds that these same Congregations have the right to fortify their particular decrees with censures, and this without any special approval, an opinion held in common with most authors, but opposed to that which Chelodi[48] and Salucci[49] hold.[50]

---

[45] Cappello, *De Censuris,* n. 11; Cavigioli, *De Censuris,* n. 7; Cerato, P., *Censurae Vigentes Ipso Facto a Codice Iuris Canonici Excerptae* (2. ed., Patavii, 1921), n. 6, 2º; Chelodi, *Ius Poenale,* n. 24 nota 1; Coronata, *Institutiones,* I, n. 335; Roberti, *De Delictis et Poenis* (Romae, 1938), n. 56; Salucci, *Il Diritto Penale secondo il Codice di Diritto Canonico* (Subiaco, 1926), p. 102, nota 1; Vermeersch-Creusen, *Epitome,* III, n. 411.

[46] *AAS,* IX (1917), 483, III.

[47] "Sacerdotes qui, his legibus non servatis, temere arroganterque demigraverint, suspensi a divinis ipso facto maneant; qui nihilominus sacris (quod Deus avertat) operari audeant, in irregularitatem incidant; a quibus poenis absolvi non possint nisi a Sacra hac Congregatione."—*AAS,* XI (1919), 43.

[48] *Ius Poenale,* n. 24 nota 1.

[49] *Diritto Penale,* p. 102, nota 1.

[50] "Chelodi dicit Congregationes Romanos, excepto S. Officio, non-nisi ex mandato Pontificis posse infligere poenas. Quod verum non est; nam, etsi decreta generalia edere nequeant nisi post approbationem R. Pontificis, ex Motu Proprio "Cum iuris canonici" Benedicti XV, 15 sept. 1917, particularia tamen decreta ferre eaque censuris munire valent."—Cappello, *De Censuris,* n. 11, nota 7.

D. The Patriarch

As in the old law, so in the new Code of Canon Law, the Patriarch as such lacks all jurisdiction in penal matters. If any coercive power is attributed to him, it is because particular law, not the general law, has granted it, or because he is an ordinary in a determined territory. Thus Canon 271 states that the title "Patriarch" does not confer any special jurisdiction unless particular law rules otherwise in some affairs. He has, however, a prerogative of honor and precedence over Metropolitans and other bishops.[51]

E. The Metropolitan

According to canon 341, § 1, bishops, either personally or through one selected by them, are obliged to conduct a visitation of their diocese at least once every five years. If they are gravely negligent in this matter, the right to undertake this canonical visitation devolves upon the Metropolitan.[52] He may not, however, enter upon this on his own authority, but must first inform the Holy See of the situation and await its approval. This supra-episcopal authority, as it were, is given by the Pope in virtue of his directive supervision of the universal Church, and as such is to be granted only in accordance with the needs of the Church.[53] The Metropolitan, therefore, can undertake this visitation, not as one jurisdictionally superior to the suffragan bishop, but rather as one vicariously empowered by the supreme authority in the Church. If this were not the case, one would be confronted with the situation that a bishop, other than the bishop of Rome, could intervene on his own authority in the jurisdiction of another. Such a procedure would be both illicit and invalid, since an individual bishop's authority is independent of every other's, save that of the Supreme Pontiff.[54]

---

[51] Cf. Cerato, *Censurae Vigentes*, n. 6, 9º; Coronata, *Institutiones*, Toso, *Commentaria Minora*, Lib. II, Tom. II, p. 95; Wernz-Vidal, *Ius Canonicum*, II, n. 526.

[52] Canon 343, § 3.

[53] Zallinger, *Institutiones Iuris Naturalis et Ecclesiastici Publici* (3 vols., Romae, 1823), III, n. 359.

[54] Ryan, *Principles of Episcopal Jurisdiction*, p. 97.

Having obtained the requisite approval, the metropolitan, when supplanting a negligent suffragan, may undertake whatever the bishop is empowered to do during a canonical visitation.[55] In case of notorious crimes[56] perpetrated before his visitation, he may punish these directly with whatever punishment he deems just, not excluding the infliction of censures.[57] In similar manner he may proceed against those who openly and notoriously commit any crime or delict against the metropolitan himself or any of his entourage. Powers other than these are not to be assumed by him, but must be obtained through a particular grant of the Supreme Pontiff.[58] This follows from the fact that the metropolitan's office is of purely ecclesiastical institution. He is therefore competent for those matters and in those circumstances only for which he is expressly empowered by the supreme authority.

F. Plenary and Provincial Councils

No bishop's jurisdiction, *per se,* extends beyond the limits of the territory over which he rules as ordinary, nor does it include any person not subject to his authority. Accordingly, bishops, when assembled in either plenary or provincial council, do not act as individual legislators, nor can their jurisdiction be considered an arithmetical cumulation of the power enjoyed by each one of them taken separately. As individual bishops they cannot obligate their equals, nor can they collegiately legislate for another.[59] They act entirely through participation of the sovereign power of the Supreme Pontiff.[60] Hence it is that, in accordance with canon 281, the permission of the Holy See must be obtained in order to convoke a plenary council, while for the holding of a provincial council the law itself bestows the necessary authoriza-

---

[55] Toso, *Commentaria Minora,* Lib. II, Tom. II, p. 98.

[56] Cf. canon 2197, nn. 2, 3.

[57] Canon 274, § 5. Cf. Cavigioli, *De Censuris,* n. 12; Chelodi, *Ius Poenale,* n. 24, nota 1; Toso, *Commentaria Minora,* Lib. II, Tom. II, p. 98.

[58] Eichmann, *Kirchenrecht,* p. 165; Wernz-Vidal, *Ius Canonicum,* II, n. 528.

[59] Chelodi, *Ius de Personis,* n. 237.

[60] Coronata, *Institutiones,* I, n. 367.

tion.[61] The opinion of Toso,[62] who holds that the power exercised by the bishops in council assembled is derived from a certain tacit pact existing among them (*ex quadam tacita pactione*) can, therefore, hardly be held.[63]

The plenary council enjoys power over the territory for which it legislates. Its competency extends, in the first place, to those things which have been outlined by the Supreme Pontiff when granting his approval, and then also to the establishing of disciplinary measures for the territory which is represented.[64] These decrees being enacted, as it were, by a superior authority are endowed with such binding force as cannot be nullified by legislation in a provincial council.[65]

The competency of a provincial council is also most ample, for to it is given legislative[66] and coercive power[67] over the province which is represented as long as this power is exercised in conformity with the common law. In disciplinary matters it can enact nothing that is opposed to the common law,[68] but it may legislate in regard to matters that are beyond (*praeter*) the common law.[69] Having this competency, both the plenary and provincial council may add such sanctions as it deems necessary to obtain the end intended.

On the conclusion of the plenary and the provincial council, the presiding officer must submit all the acts and decrees to the Holy See and these shall not be promulgated until the Sacred Congregation of the Council has considered and approved them.[70] This submission of the acts and decrees of the council is required

---

[61] Canon 283.

[62] *Commentaria Minora,* Lib. II, Tom. II, p. 178.

[63] Chelodi, *Ius de Personis,* n. 237.

[64] Wernz-Vidal, *Ius Canonicum,* II, n. 539.

[65] Toso, *Commentaria Minora,* Lib. II, Tom. I, p. 110.

[66] Conc. Trid., sess. XXIV, *de ref.,* c. 2.

[67] Conc. Trid., sess. XXIV, *de ref.,* c. 5; Bouix, *Tractatus de Concilio Provinciali* (2. ed., Parisiis, 1862), 469-471.

[68] S. C. Conc. 19 feb. 1921—*AAS,* XIII (1921), 228.

[69] S. C. Conc. 11 dec. 1920—*AAS,* XIII (1921), 350.

[70] Canon 291, § 1. Councils held in territories subject to the Congregation for the Propagation of the Faith must submit the decrees to this Congregation.—Canon 304, § 2.

before they can be licitly and validly promulgated.[71] The approval granted by the Holy See does not make these decrees pontifical nor are they made binding on the universal church, unless the Holy See declares otherwise, but rather an inspection is made to determine whether or not a certain decree is too severe or perhaps inopportune.[72]

G. *Vicars and Prefects Apostolic, Abbots and Prelates Nullius*

Vicars and Prefects Apostolic, as also Abbots and Prelates *nullius,* rule over territories which are exempted from the jurisdiction of residential bishops, and which, in themselves, have not yet been erected into dioceses.[73] The jurisdiction which they exercise is ordinary, being annexed to the very office which they hold.[74] As *Ordinarii* and *Ordinarii locorum* of canon 198, they have all the rights and faculties which the Code gives to Ordinaries; thus they can be truly said to exercise a quasi-episcopal power over the territory assigned them.[75] In addition, canons 294, § 1, and 323, § 1, give them, in the territory over which they rule, the same rights and faculties which are enjoyed by residential bishops, unless the Holy See makes special reservations. In view of this, Vicars and Prefects Apostolic, Abbots and Prelates *nullius,* have

---

[71] Eichmann, *Kirchenrecht,* p. 168; Wernz-Vidal, *Ius Canonicum,* II, n. 540.

[72] Benedict XIV, *De Synodo Dioecesana,* Lib. XIII, cap. 3, nn. 3, 4, 5. "A National or Provincial Council may be ratified by the Holy See in two ways: a) *In forma communi,* when the decrees are not examined separately, nor approved *motu proprio* and *ex certa scientia.* b) *In forma specifica,* when all the acts and decrees are carefully reviewed and confirmed *motu proprio* and *ex certa scientia.* The approbation *in forma communi* adds no authority whatever to the decrees of National Councils, while that *in forma specifica* gives them the force of universal laws of the Church."—Cicognani, *Canon Law* (Authorized English version by J. O'Hara and F. Brennan, Philadelphia: Dolphin Press, 1934), p. 553, nota 7; cf. Coronata, *Institutiones,* I, p. 440, nota 7; Van Hove, *Commentarium Lovaniense in Codicem Iuris Canonici,* Vol. II, *De Legibus Ecclesiasticis* (Mechliniae: H. Dessain, 1930), pp. 349-350, n. 342.

[73] Canons 293, § 1; 319, § 1.

[74] Canon 197. Cf. Chelodi, *Ius de Personis,* n. 183; Vermeersch-Creusen, *Epitome,* I, n. 404; Wernz-Vidal, *Ius Canonicum,* II, n. 544.

[75] Coronata, *Institutiones,* I, nn. 372, 389.

the right and duty to govern their territories in temporal and spiritual matters, and therefore they have legislative, judicial and coercive powers. Thus they may enact or abrogate laws for their territory; they may issue precepts, and they may enforce their laws and precepts with whatever measures they deem fitting, even with the use of censures.[76]

The Sacred Congregation for the Propagation of the Faith on February 14, 1702, declared that a Vicar Apostolic could exercise jurisdiction only within the confines of the territory entrusted to him by the Holy See in his letter of appointment. Contrariwise, no other bishop or Ordinary, although he be a metropolitan, or any dignitary whatsoever, could presume to exercise jurisdiction in those places which were ruled by a Vicar Apostolic.[77] This reservation of jurisdiction to the Vicar Apostolic and this exemption from the interference of any other Ordinary are applicable also to the Prefect Apostolic and to the Abbot and Prelate *nullius*.

Within the territory of the vicariate or prefecture apostolic or of the abbacy or prelacy *nullius*, all missionaries, even regulars, are subject to the jurisdiction, visitation and correction of the *Ordinarius loci*.[78] Those who are not religious are subject to the same extent that clerics are subject to their respective bishops, while religious are subject in the things pertaining to the government of the mission, the care of souls, and the administration of the sacraments, in accordance with the rules of Canon Law.[79]

H. Apostolic Administrator

Canon 312 states that the Administrator Apostolic may be appointed for sees which already have their Ordinaries as well as

---

[76] Chelodi, *Ius de Personis*, n. 183; Coronata, *Institutiones*, I, n. 373; Eichmann, *Kirchenrecht*, p. 170; Toso, *Commentaria Minora*, pp. 155, 147; Wernz-Vidal, *Ius Canonicum*, II, nn. 545, 569; Winslow, *Vicars and Prefects Apostolic* (The Catholic University of America, Canon Law Studies, n. 24, Washington, D. C.: The Catholic University of America, 1924), p. 15.

[77] *Collectanea S. C. P. F.*, n. 253.

[78] Canon 296, § 1.

[79] Eichmann, *Kirchenrecht*, p. 171; Wernz-Vidal, *Ius Canonicum*, II, n. 546; Winslow, *Vicars and Prefects Apostolic*, p. 18.

for sees which are vacant, but in all instances the appointment is made only for special and grave reasons. Hence, if a bishop, through old age, infirmity, physical or mental debility, is unable to discharge properly the functions of his office, or if serious financial, religious or political difficulties arise in a diocese and cannot be controlled by the bishop, it may be expected that the Holy See will appoint an Administrator Apostolic to administer the see.[80] It follows, therefore, that the Administrator is a true ordinary in the canonical sense of the term,[81] although, being appointed by direct commission of the Supreme Pontiff and being subject to removal at the command of the same, he exercises ordinary jurisdiction only vicariously and not in his own name.[82]

Once he is properly appointed to a diocese, the Apostolic Administrator governs in the manner specified in his decree of appointment; if his appointment is permanent, he has the same powers as a residential bishop, and if it is temporary, his powers are those of the Vicar Capitular or Administrator.[83] This jurisdiction comprises legislative, judicial and coercive powers as predicated of these respective offices. Hence, in penal matters, he enjoys that jurisdiction which is necessary properly to carry out the office to which he has been assigned, and he exercises this jurisdiction as ordinary, not at delegated, power.

ARTICLE III. EPISCOPAL JURISDICTION IN THE CHURCH

A. The Bishop

By divine institution there are two degrees in the ecclesiastical hierarchy of jurisdiction: the primacy of the Roman Pontiff and the episcopate.[84] Just as there must always be bishops in the

---

[80] Eichmann, *Kirchenrecht*, p. 174; Vermeersch-Creusen, *Epitome*, I, n. 431; Wernz-Vidal, *Ius Canonicum*, II, n. 557.

[81] Canon 198, § 1.

[82] Canon 197, § 2. Cf. Eichmann, *Kirchenrecht*, 174; Toso, *Commentaria Minora*, Lib. II, Tom. II, p. 138; Wernz-Vidal, *Ius Canonicum*, II, n. 557.

[83] Canon 315.

[84] Conc. Vat., Sess. IV, cap. 3—*Coll. Lac.*, VII, 269; Bouix, *Tractatus de Episcopo ubi et de Synodo Dioecesana* (2. ed., 2 vols., Parisiis, 1873), I, 104.

Church to provide for its spiritual ministry, so there must also be bishops, distinct from the pope, to govern it.[85] Although jurisdictionally subordinate to the Supreme Pontiff, inasmuch as his jurisdiction is derived not from God immediately but from the Pontiff as its proximate cause,[86] the bishop's power is circumscribed by no limits of human law save those of the general law of the Church and the particular decrees issued by the pope.[87]

The jurisdiction which the bishop exercises is *ordinary*,[88] a power that is not entrusted to him personally but officially.[89] It is not a power that is merely delegated to him by another. He is, therefore, not the delegate of anyone, whether within or without the Church,[90] nor can he be looked upon as the vicar of the pope in the ordinary conduct of his diocese.[91] The jurisdiction which he possesses is not to be used *per modum actus,* in certain circumstances or under certain conditions only, but is such as is necessary for the daily conduct of the diocese. The bishop also acts *immediately,* inasmuch as there is no divinely ordained minister through whom he must exercise his jurisdiction,[92] and therefore he is empowered to act directly independent of any other power, secular or clerical.[93]

Mere election, designation or presentation of a candidate is not sufficient for the exercise of the episcopal jurisdiction, but there is required the appointment to a particular diocese by the Roman

---

85 Toso, *Commentaria Minora,* Lib. II, Tom. II, p. 151.

86 Pius VI, const. "*Caritas,*" 13 apr. 1791, § 18—*Fontes,* n. 474; Pesch, *Praelect. Dogmaticae,* Lib. I, tit. I, n. 39; Wernz-Vidal, *Ius Canonicum,* II, n. 579.

87 "Praeterquam generalibus Ecclesiae legibus ac peculiaribus R. Pontificum decretis, nullis limitibus circumscribitur."—*Jus Pont.,* IV (1924), 10.

88 Canon 339, § 1.

89 Eichmann, *Kirchenrecht,* p. 177; Ryan, *Principles of Episcopal Jurisdiction,* p. 51; Vermeersch-Creusen, *Epitome,* III, n. 449.

90 Canon 197, § 1; Bouix, *De Episcopo,* I, 104.

91 Leo XIII, ep. encycl. "*Satis cognitum,*" 29 iun. 1896, n. 25—*Fontes,* n. 630.

92 Conc. Vat. Sess. IV, cap. 3—*Coll. Lac.,* VII, 269.

93 Pius IX, litt. encyc. "*Etsi multa,*" 20 nov. 1873—*Fontes,* n. 566; Leo XIII, ep. encyc. "*Immortale Dei,*" 1 nov. 1855—*Fontes,* n. 592; Pius X, litt. encyc. "*Iamdudum,*" 24 maii 1911—*Fontes,* n. 692.

Pontiff and the subsequent institution as ordinary of that diocese.[94] Although the individual may not as yet have been consecrated, he may take possession of the diocese as soon as he receives the apostolic letters of appointment;[95] once he has taken canonical possession, he has the full jurisdictional powers of that office and may exercise them either directly or through another.[96]

In view of the purpose of his office, the bishop must be granted such jurisdictional powers as are necessary for the good government of the diocese assigned him.[97] By divine right he is guardian and shepherd of the flock entrusted to his care, and therefore must possess the powers required for the fulfillment of this charge, legislative, judicial and coercive. Episcopal laws have *per se* all the characteristics of particular positive law. There is no confirmation required on the part of a higher authority,[98] although the Supreme Pontiff may establish conditions for the use of episcopal jurisdiction, and may even restrict it, yet all the time merely reserving to himself without denying to the bishop certain aspects of truly legislative power.[99] It may be said then that the residential bishop's legislative jurisdiction is contained within the limits of the common or papal law and that thus diocesan legislation may be a positive and particular determinant of a general law in full accordance with it (*secundum ius*); it may even extend to matters not legislated upon in the common law and therefore go beyond it (*praeter ius*), but it can never be of a character that opposes the common law (*contra ius*).[100] Whether acting in synod or independently thereof the bishop is the sole lawgiver in his diocese.[101] Being thus legislatively em-

---

[94] Canon 332, § 1.

[95] Coronata, *Institutiones,* I, n. 393, 6o b.

[96] Canon 334, § 1. Cf. Cappello, *De Censuris,* n. 11; Wernz-Vidal, *Ius Canonicum,* II, nn. 579, 581.

[97] Ottaviani, *Institutiones Iuris Publici Eccl.,* I, n. 220.

[98] Benedict XIV, *De Synodo Dioecesana,* lib. XIII, c. 3, n. 6; Wernz-Vidal, *Ius Canonicum,* II, n. 599; Coronata, *Institutiones,* I, n. 414.

[99] See discussion of "causae maiores" in Article I of this chapter.

[100] Vermeersch-Creusen, *Epitome,* III, n. 450, 1o; Wernz-Vidal, *Ius Canonicum,* II, n. 599.

[101] Canon 362.

powered, he can also issue precepts or enact personal laws governing those who are his subjects.[102]

The authority of the bishop, however, regards not merely the enactment of the law but also the application thereof, and therefore he is not only the divinely appointed teacher of doctrine, but also the divinely ordained ruler of conduct and regulator of discipline. Having enacted a law or issued a precept, he is likewise empowered to annex thereto proper measures or penalties which will ensure their observance. Thus the bishop enjoys full coercive powers in his diocese, whether in regard to the application of penalties designated in the common law or whether in regard to the conduct of right order through immediate disciplinary and penal decrees.[103]

ARTICLE IV. PARTICIPANTS IN THE EPISCOPAL JURISDICTION IN THE CHURCH

A. Vicar Capitular or Administrator

Only when a diocese is vacant does the Board of Consultors and later the Administrator enter upon their office. Canon 430, § 1, states that the episcopal see becomes vacant on the death of the bishop, on his resignation accepted by the Roman Pontiff, on his transfer, and on his deprivation of office authentically communicated to him. Once the see is fully vacant, the administration of the diocese ordinarily passes to the Board of Diocesan Consultors or to the Chapter[104] unless other provisions exist.[105]

---

[102] Wernz-Vidal, *Ius Canonicum,* II, 599 I.

[103] Canon 335, § 1. Chelodi, *Ius de Personis,* p. 311.

[104] Canon 431, § 1; Coronata, *Institutiones,* I, n. 461; Jaeger, *The Administration of Vacant and Quasi-Vacant Dioceses in the United States* (Catholic University of America, Canon Law Studies, n. 81, Washington, D. C.: The Catholic University of America, 1932), n. 88 sq.; Klekotka, *Diocesan Consultors* (The Catholic University of America, Canon Law Studies, n. 8, Washington, D. C.: The Catholic University of America, 1920), p. 86 sq.; Wernz-Vidal, *Ius Canonicum,* II, n. 709.

[105] Such other provisions may be the appointment of an Apostolic Administrator; the existence of a Coadjutor with right of succession; the transfer of a bishop who, because of his transfer by the Holy See, becomes administrator of the diocese where formerly he was the ordinary.

The Board of Consultors or the Chapter is consequently the successor of the bishop, and as such has the right and duty to provide for the administration of the diocese, and is termed the *ordinarius loci.*[106] By a distinct grant the law endows the Board or the Chapter with the ordinary jurisdiction of the bishop, thereby empowering it to do all that the bishop can do in view of his ordinary jurisdiction, excepting those things expressly forbidden in law.[107] These powers are possessed by the Board or the Chapter as such, and not by the individual members who unite to form this college.[108] By the very disposition of the law itself, therefore, the Board of Consultors or the Chapter possesses ordinary and not delegated episcopal jurisdiction. It becomes the successor of the bishop. In consequence of this, it may exercise the legislative, judicial and coercive rights of the bishop by force of ordinary episcopal jurisdiction which the law has conceded to it.

Within the definite time specified by law[109] the Board or the Chapter must proceed to the selection of the Vicar Capitular or Administrator. The ordinary episcopal jurisdiction which the Board or the Chapter receives when the see becomes vacant passes in its entirety to the Vicar or the Administrator once he is properly designated and the office is accepted;[110] his election or appointment, therefore, establishes him as the successor of the bishop and the sole possessor of ordinary episcopal jurisdiction in the vacant see for all jurisdictional matters concerning which the law of the Church has not indicated an express exception or a certain prohibition.[111] Being the successor of the bishop, he is known as

---

[106] Canons 431, § 1; 198.

[107] Canon 435.

[108] Cappello, *Summa Iuris,* I, n. 475; Coronata, *Institutiones,* I, n. 451; Vermeersch-Creusen, *Epitome,* I, n. 520; Wernz-Vidal, *Ius Canonicum,* II, n. 198.

[109] Canon 432, § 1.

[110] Canon 435, § 1.

[111] Canon 435, § 1; Pius IX, const. *"Romanus Pontifex,"* 28 aug. 1873—*Fontes,* n. 565; cf. Ayrinhac, *Constitution of the Church in the New Code of Canon Law* (New York, 1925), p. 275; Cocchi, *Commentarium in Codicem Iuris Canonici* (8 vols., Taurini, 1931-1940), III (3. ed., 1931), n. 321.

the *Ordinarius loci*[112] and as a consequence the object, the limitations and the mode of the exercise of his jurisdiction are governed by the same rules that are applicable to the bishop. Hence, just as the bishop, so the Vicar or Administrator enjoys legislative, judicial and coercive powers which he may exercise over every one of his subjects.[113] Obviously the power of legislating includes the capacity to issue precepts which affect individual persons. Since the Vicar or Administrator possesses the power to make laws, to impose precepts and to judge, he may also attach penalties to his laws and precepts.[114] He may, consequently, inflict various penalties, including censures, on all violators of the divine or ecclesiastical, general or particular law, and do all things necessary for correction, right order and discipline, just as the bishop himself can do within the limits of his ordinary jurisdiction.

B. The Vicar-General

All authors are agreed that the Vicar-General does not have the power to annex any penalty to a precept that he may give.[115] Blat[116] is very explicit in his statement regarding this, for he says that in virtue of the limitation expressed in canon 2220, § 2, the Vicar-General does not have the power to annex penalties whether medicinal or vindictive, nor can he punish with a penalty any transgression of the law. Chelodi[117] understands the word "inflict" (*infligendi*) of the canon in the sense of "enact" (*sta-*

---

[112] Canon 198.

[113] Cf. Canons 335, 336; Cappello, *Summa Iuris,* I, n. 402; Cocchi, *Commentarium,* III, n. 321; Sipos, *Enchiridion Juris Canonici* (Pecs, 1926), p. 287.

[114] Cappello, *De Censuris,* n. 11; De Meester, *Iuris Canonici et Iuris Canonico-Civilis Compendium* (3 vols. in 4, Brugis, 1921-1928), Tomus III, Pars II, n. 1770; Vermeersch-Creusen, *Epitome,* III, n. 411.

[115] Blat, *Commentarium Textus Codicis Iuris Canonici* (5 vols. in 6, Romae, 1921-1927), VI, n. 38; Chelodi, *Ius Poenale,* n. 24; Coronata, *Institutiones,* IV, n. 1693; Pistocchi, "De Superiore Potestatem Coactivam Habente," *Il Monitore Ecclesiastico,* IX (1937), p. 13; Salucci, *Diritto Penale,* p. 99; Sole, *De Delictis et Poenis* (Romae, 1920), n. 83; Wernz-Vidal, *Ius Canonicum,* VII, n. 165.

[116] *Loc. cit.*

[117] *Ius Poenale,* n. 24 nota 2.

tuendi) and thus denies this power to the Vicar-General.[118] Coronata, however, understands the word, not in this limited sense, but in the wider sense of enacting and inflicting, and thus denies to the Vicar-General the power of either enacting a penal law or subjecting a delinquent to a penalty determined in law.[119] Salucci[120] holds similarly, stating that the Vicar-General is not able to enact a penalty, and can apply a penalty only when delegated, and this only for an individual case (*caso per caso*). Sole[121] finds the reason why the Vicar-General cannot inflict a penalty in the fact that he is not a judge, but Coronata[122] disagrees with this, for he states that the infliction of a penalty does not necessarily demand the office of the judge. He finds the reason in the fact that this canon requires a mandate, because there is question here of something of great moment.

Briefly, then, it may be stated that the Vicar-General cannot annex a penalty to any law or precept and cannot subject a delinquent to any penalty without first having received a special mandate.

C. *The Officialis or Judge*

Although the Code states in canon 2220, § 1, that the judge can merely impose by the process of law the penalties legitimately attached to a law or precept, there are certain cases in which the Code expressly sanctions a different procedure, and there is then given to the *Officialis* or judge not merely the faculty of applying penalties but also that of annexing penalties to precepts or of inflicting them in the strict sense.[123] Thus the judge is permitted to use measures deemed fitting, even the infliction of censures, when there is question of restoring the obedience and respect

---

[118] Salucci, *Diritto Penale,* p. 94 nota 1, erroneously states that Chelodi grants this power to the Vicar General.

[119] ". . . non potest, ne valide quidem, poenas legi aut praecepto a se dato adnectere; nec sententia condemnatoria reum poenae a iure latae subiicere." —*Institutiones,* IV, n. 1693, p. 84.

[120] *Diritto Penale,* p. 99, nota 1.

[121] *De Delictis et Poenis,* n. 83.

[122] *Institutiones,* IV, n. 1693, p. 84, nota 4.

[123] Coronata, *Institutiones,* IV, n. 1693, p. 85, nota 1.

necessary in a court of law.[124] So also if a witness does not appear when summoned, unless he be excused, or if he appears, but refuses to answer, to take the oath, or to sign his name to his testimony, he may be punished with appropriate penalties.[125] Finally, the judge is permitted to threaten and to inflict ecclesiastical penalties when the defendant is found contumacious.[126]

At first sight there seems to be an evident contradiction between canon 2220, § 1, and the above cited canons which permit the judge to inflict penalties as he finds necessary. Noval considers these canons exceptions to the law stated in canon 2220, § 1, and maintains that the judge, in view of the very nature of his office, does possess a certain coercive power.[127] With this view Vermeersch-Creusen seemingly agree.[128] Salucci, however, does not agree.[129] He maintains, less correctly, that this power by which the Code empowers the judge to inflict penalties must not be confused with that which other ecclesiastical superiors possess in virtue of their office (*iure proprio*), but is a simple delegation made by the Code of that power which is required by the judge properly to exercise the duties of his office.

Whichever opinion is accepted, the fact still remains, that the judge has the power to inflict penalties, including censures, in the cases specified in law.[130]

---

[124] Canon 1640, § 2.

[125] Canon 1766, § 2.

[126] Canon 1845.

[127] "Et ex hoc satis innuit competere suapse natura judici aliquam potestatem coercitivam."—*Commentarius Codicis Iuris Canonici Libri IV de Processibus* (2 vols., Romae, 1920), I, *De Iudiciis*, n. 219.

[128] "Cum Codex iudici potestatem faciat in quibusdam casibus partes vel alias personas decretis seu praeceptis iurisdictionalibus ad aliquid faciendum vel omittendum cogendi, vi ipsius c. 2220 iudex potest decretis seu praeceptis poenam annectere."—*Epitome*, III, n. 216, 2o.

[129] *Diritto Penale*, pp. 97-98.

[130] The term "Bishop," "Ordinary," or "Superior," when used hereafter in this treatise, will include all the foregoing, with the limitations expressed in the respective considerations.

CHAPTER VII

Subject of Coercive Powers of Superiors

ARTICLE I. THOSE HAVING DOMICILE OR QUASI-DOMICILE

Canon 2226, § 1, states that all those who are bound by a certain law or precept are also bound by the penalty annexed thereto. Law is a rule and measure for the acts of subjects, and a person becomes its subject through having a domicile or quasi-domicile in a particular territory, and not by the sole fact of physical residence or sojourn in a given locality as long as a domicile or quasi-domicile is maintained elsewhere.[1]

Those who have established a domicile within a definite territory (*incolae*) are evidently those who are permanently subject to the jurisdiction of an ecclesiastical superior. They are the usual and ordinary subjects of a superior's jurisdiction, unless they have been exempted therefrom through a special privilege.[2] Among those who are naturally subject to diocesan laws and who are permanent subjects of the perceptive powers of the superior, there is no essential difference between clerical and lay, religious and secular.[3] Of these, the diocesan clergy are the most permanent subjects, for they cannot, as the laity, withdraw themselves from one territory to another, but are held by an additional bond, that of incardination.[4]

For the acquiring of a domicile two things must be considered: residence in a diocese or territory, and the intention of remaining there. When the intention to remain permanently is had, then a domicile can be acquired without continued residence; a very limited sojourn accompanied with this intention suffices. When

---

[1] Cicognani, *Canon Law*, p. 575.

[2] Benedict XIV, *De Synodo Dioecesana*, Lib. XIII, cap. 5, n. 5; Meysztowicz, "Domicilium et Quasi-Domicilium Eorumque Effectus in Codice Juris Canonici"—*Jus Pont.*, VI (1926), 112, 155.

[3] Sole, *De Delictis et Poenis*, n. 104.

[4] Canon 111. Cf. S. C. C., 12 aug. 1871—*ASS*, VI (1870), 587.

the intention is not had, then a continued residence of at least ten years is necessary to effect automatically the establishment of a domicile in a particular locality.[5] A quasi-domicile, on the other hand, is acquired by residence in a diocese with the intention of staying there for the greater part of the year unless something calls one away, or by having actually lived there for the greater part of the year.[6] The mere change of residence within a diocese does not cause the loss of domicile or quasi-domicile, nor does it beget exemption from the coercive jurisdiction of the superior of that territory; only an actual transfer of domicile or quasi-domicile from the diocese or territory can effect this. As regards the observance of law or precept and the subsequent liability to the penalties annexed thereto, there is no practical distinction between domicile and quasi-domicile, as long as one is actually present in either of these territories.[7]

This binding force of and subjection to laws and precepts because of actual physical presence in a territory exists also in the case of *vagi,* that is, of those having neither a domicile nor quasi-domicile.[8] In this instance the jurisdiction exercised over them by the superior is both territorial and temporary; territorial because it is occasioned by and made dependent upon their actual presence in the diocese; temporary, because their presence is merely transitory, in as far as there is no definitely abiding band which links their residence with the locality. During their stay in the diocese, the bishop's coercive jurisdiction over them is as complete and extensive as it is in regard to habitual or permanent subjects.[9]

It may be useful to consider here also the status of those religious, who formerly were completely subject to the jurisdiction of a religious superior, but who at the present moment are temporarily authorized by indult to reside out of their monastery or religious house. Such an indult implies the status of a

---

[5] Canon 92, § 1.

[6] Canon 92, § 2.

[7] Cicognani, *Canon Law,* p. 576.

[8] Canon 91.

[9] Van Hove, *De Legibus,* n. 224.

probationary service under the vigilance of the diocesan ordinary. It renders such a religious subject in his obedience, even by the additional duty engendered by his vow, to this ecclesiastical superior, just as a lay person is made subject in view of his domicile or quasi-domicile.[10] Hence, during the interim such a religious is withdrawn from the jurisdiction of the religious superior and becomes subject to the ordinary of the place in which he now resides. One who is secularized must return to the diocese to which he has continuously belonged, if the link binding him to that diocese was not severed through perpetual profession; if the bond was severed, he may be accepted immediately by a bishop without any previous period of probation. By such an absolute and unconditional acceptation, the religious immediately becomes incardinated in the diocese and henceforth shares the status of a diocesan cleric as represented in the indult granting permanent secularization.[11] The bishop, however, may subject such a religious to a period of probation. This period may be extended to three full years, at the end of which time it may be continued for another three years; if the religious is not dismissed at the end of that time, he is *"ipso facto"* incardinated in the diocese, and his status is that of a diocesan cleric.[12] Such a one, then, in view of his incardination is subject to the diocesan ordinary in penal matters just as is a member of the laity in virtue of a domicile.

Finally there must be considered the relation existing between the ecclesiastical superior and those absent from the territory in which they possess their domicile or quasi-domicile. Generally, one who is physically and morally absent from the place of domicile or quasi-domicile is not bound by its laws, for ordinarily a law is territorial and immediately affects those domiciled and actually residing there.[13] As a result, although the ecclesiastical

---

[10] Canon 639.

[11] Canon 641, § 2. Cf. Schaefer, *De Religiosis ad Normam Codicis Iuris Canonici* (Muenster, 1927), p. 574.

[12] Canon 641.

[13] Cappello, *De Censuris*, n. 15; Coronata, *Institutiones*, I, n. 15; Ferreres, *Compendium Theologiae Moralis ad Normam Codicis Canonici* (2 vols., Bacrinone, 1920), I, n. 160; Sole, *De Delictis et Poenis*, n. 104; Wernz,

superior in a particular territory may have enacted a law and annexed a penalty to be incurred *ipso facto* for its violation, a subject violating that law while absent from the territory of his ordinary could not ordinarily be held liable to the penalty. Hence, the jurisdiction of the superior would be restricted, as it were, in this particular instance. There may be, however, personal or extraterritorial laws which directly and immediately affect a person, independently of any territory where he may be. Territoriality is not an essential quality of law, for law is primarily the regulator of human acts.[14] Hence there is no reason why a legitimate superior, although he exercises jurisdiction over a determinate territory, should not be able to enact truly personal laws which bind subjects who may be temporarily absent from their diocesan domicile, for, although they be absent, they still remain under the jurisdiction of the superior of the territory where they have their domicile or quasi-domicile.[15]

Legislative power and the right to annex penalties pertains to voluntary jurisdiction, and therefore, according to canon 201, § 3, may be exercised by a superior on subjects even though they be absent from the territory over which he rules. Accordingly, those laws are considered personal which are enacted for a community essentially personal, as, for instance, laws pertaining to exempt religious; or which concern the juridical state and quality of persons, as a law requiring certain conditions before a cleric may be ordained; or those which impose an essentially personal obligation, as a law which demands the wearing of a certain garb by the clergy of a diocese. Finally there are those laws which a bishop may declare as binding his subjects when they are absent from his territory, as the frequenting of theatres, and the reading of specified books. Such laws must not be considered territorial. Their binding force within a determined and defined area suggests a territorial limitation, yet the very nature of the

---

Ius Decretalium, I, n. 107; VI, n. 151; Wernz-Vidal, *Ius Canonicum,* VII, n. 228; I, n. 153.

[14] St. Thomas, *Summa Theologica,* Pars Prima-Secundae, q. 90, art. 1; Cicognani, *Canon Law,* p. 546; Maroto, *Institutiones,* I, n. 183.

[15] Michiels, *Normae Generales Iuris Canonici* (2 vols., Lublin-Polonia, 1929), I, 308.

general precept indicates that it begets a personal obligation in each member of a certain community or class. Although it is only one law, in effect it is multiple, for it assumes the nature of a personal precept and therefore, according to canon 24, binds each individual even when he is absent from his domicile.[16] As the subject is bound to the performance or the omission of a certain act specified in the law, so also is he liable to the penalty designated in that law for its violation.

Another instance in which a superior could exercise his coercive powers even though the subject is actually absent from his territory is had when the subject commits a transgression which does harm in his own territory.[17] In such a case, by a fiction of law, a person can be said to be morally present in his own territory, because of the effect which his transgression has produced; hence such laws would be considered territorial in respect to their observance, but personal as to their obligation.[18] Absent subjects, therefore, are bound by all laws and penalties annexed thereto, as enacted by the superior, which concern an office which they have undertaken, a benefice which they possess, and by all measures that are similarly intended to promote the common good. Just as these subjects are affected by laws enacted prior to their departure, so also are they affected by penalties imposed by the superior by way of precept. Thus, the violation of the law of residence, the fulfillment of an obligation connected with an office or a benefice or any other services demanded in a particular territory, the writing of articles to be printed in magazines prohibited by particular legislation, these and other similar acts or omissions of a subject absent from his own territory, make that subject liable to the penal laws or precepts enacted or issued by his ecclesiastical

---

[16] Michiels, *Normae Generales,* I, 520.

[17] Canon 14, § 1, n. 1.

[18] Cappello, *De Censuris,* n. 19; Coronata, *Institutiones,* I, n. 15; Cicognani, *Canon Law,* p. 581; De Meester, *Compendium,* III, n. 1713; Ferreres, *Compendium,* I, n. 160; Genicot,—Salsmans, *Institutiones Theologiae Moralis* (11. ed., 2 vols., Bruxellis, 1927), II, n. 567; Noldin-Schmitt, *Summa Theol. Moral.,* I, n. 152; Roberti, *De Delictis et Poenis,* n. 60; Sole, *De Delictis et Poenis,* n. 106; Van Hove, *De Legibus,* n. 209; Wernz, *Ius Decretalium,* VI, n. 151; Wernz-Vidal, *Ius Canonicum,* VII, 238-239.

superior, for they are considered as injurious to the common good of the territory to which he belongs.

Finally, the question of change of domicile or jurisdiction may be considered as it affects the exercise of coercive powers when a penalty is merely threatened. After one has changed his domicile, if he commits a transgression that was prohibited under pain of censure by his former ecclesiastical superior, that superior cannot inflict or demand the observance of that censure, whether it was annexed to a law or to a general or particular precept, for through the change of domicile one ceases to be the subject of his former ecclesiastical superior, even as regards personal precept.[19] If a precept, having annexed thereto a *ferendae sententiae* censure, is imposed upon a subject, the change of domicile or entrance into a religious Order before the imposition of the censure will free the transgressor of the liability of incurring it. Thus, if a superior says to one of his subjects: "If you do that again, I shall excommunicate you," then the change of domicile will remove the liability of incurring the censure threatened.[20] On the other hand, should a judge declare that unless a contumacious party appears within a specified time he will be automatically excommunicated, that party would be liable to the censure even though he changed his domicile, for the sentence has been pronounced, although its execution remains suspended pending the fulfillment or non-fulfillment of the condition within the specified time.[21] If, however, a censure is conditionally inflicted with reference to something in the past which was done at a time when a domicile was had in the territory of the superior imposing the censure, then a change of domicile will not free a person from the liability of incurring that censure; thus, a superior may state: "Unless you restore the stolen things within one month, you will be excom-

[19] Cappello, *De Censuris*, n. 19; Wernz, *Ius Decretalium*, VI, n. 151, nota 55; Wernz-Vidal, *Ius Canonicum*, VII, 238, nota 42; Meysztowicz, "Domicilium et Quasi-Domicilium . . . ," *Jus Pont.*, VI (1926), 115.

[20] Suarez, *Opera Omnia* (ed. Lucovicus Vives, 26 vols., Parisiis, 1861), XXIII, *De Censuris in Communi*, disp. III, sec. V, n. 2.

[21] D'Annibale, *Summula Theologiae Moralis* (5. ed., 3 vols., Romae, 1908), I, 333; Lega, *De Delictis et Poenis*, n. 111; Suarez, *loc. cit.*

municated," and then the change of domicile before the lapse of that time will not free the subject from the obligation imposed.[22]

ARTICLE II. TRANSIENTS

The ecclesiastical superior of a territory is entrusted with the well-being and the good order of those subject to him, and therefore, as he is empowered to legislate for them, so also is he empowered to annex penalties for the violation of his laws.[23] It is a fundamental principle of law, however, that the power of jurisdiction can be exercised directly only upon those who are subjects.[24] What power, then, has the ordinary over those who are not his subjects, but who are transients in his territory? Generally considered, transients—those who are absent from the place of their domicile or quasi-domicile[25] cannot be considered the subjects of the ecclesiastical superior in whose territory they sojourn, and hence he cannot exercise coercive powers over them. Maroto[26] contends that those who have jurisdiction in a definite territory are able to determine the conditions in accordance with which transients are permitted to enter or remain within their territory and that these transients must submit to the sanctions imposed unless they are willing to comply with the specified conditions. This general affirmation evidently cannot be accepted, for canon 14, § 1, n. 2, states that transients are bound by those laws only which deal with matters of public order (*"ordini publico consulunt"*) or which determine the formalities of certain acts (*"actuum sollemnia determinant"*). There is no power granted in the common law by which the ordinary can indiscriminately determine the conditions in accordance with which transients, both

[22] Cappello, *De Censuris*, n. 119; Suarez, *De Censuris*, disp. III, sec. V, n. 5; Wernz, *Ius Decretalium*, VI, n. 151, nota 55; Wernz-Vidal, *Ius Canonicum*, VII, p. 238, nota 42.

[23] Canon 2220, § 1.

[24] Canon 201, § 1.

[25] Canon 91.

[26] *Institutiones*, I, n. 201, nota 2; cf. also Lehmkuhl, *Theologia Moralis* (10. ed., 2 vols., Friburgi Brisgoviae, 1902), I, n. 141.

lay and clerical, may enter into his territory.[27] Accordingly, he may not forbid the stay of any of the laity, and may act against a cleric for a just cause only,[28] for the prohibition to remain in a certain place is an ecclesiastical penalty, and penalties may be imposed only when a delict has been committed.[29] Again, a local ordinary may not enact a particular law for certain transients simply because a similar law exists in the place of their domicile, for in the place of domicile the end intended may easily be such as does not involve public order.[30]

A superior, therefore, is not prohibited from enacting laws which are obligatory upon transients, as long as they are not opposed to the prescriptions of the *ius commune*.[31] The only condition under which he may so legislate, as already pointed out, is when there is question of the public order. Just what constitutes a law enacted for the protection of public order has been much disputed. There are certain authors[32] who hold that transients are bound by all penal laws existing in the place of their sojourn, for, they say, penal laws are always enacted to promote the common good. Seemingly they base their opinion on a law of the Decretals,[33] which states that when a delict is committed by a transient, the judge of the place is competent *"ratione delicti."* This indeed determines judicial competency after a delict has been committed, but it does not state just what constitutes a delict on the part of the transient; hence, another basis for this obligation must be sought.[34]

The general consensus is that those laws concern the public order which tend to avoid a common danger, such as scandal and

---

[27] Michiels, *Normae Generales,* p. 322; Van Hove, *De Legibus,* n. 218.

[28] Canon 144.

[29] Canon 2298, n. 7.

[30] Van Hove, *De Legibus,* n. 218.

[31] Cappello, *Summa Iuris Canonici,* I, n. 80; Michiels, *Normae Generales,* p. 321; Wernz, *Ius Decretalium,* I, n. 107; Wernz-Vidal, *Ius Canonicum,* I, n. 156.

[32] Cocchi, *Commentarium,* I, n. 56; Maroto, *Institutiones,* I, n. 201; Roberti, *De Delictis et Poenis,* n. 60; Toso, *Commentaria Minora,* I, 31; Meysztowicz, "Domicilium et Quasi-Domicilium . . . ," *Ius Pont.,* VI (1926), 155.

[33] C. 20, X, *de foro competenti,* II, 2.

[34] Michiels, *Normae Generales,* p. 322.

harm to the inhabitants.[85] Vermeersch-Creusen well explain the passage by saying that it includes those laws which tend to avert a common danger rather than those tending directly to the promotion of the common good.[86] The question, then, is not whether the observance of a particular law will be to the positive advantage of the community, but rather whether the transgression of the law will be harmful to the community either in its government or in regard to measures of safety and security. Transients are not bound to work for the good of the community, but they are not permitted to bring harm through their non-observance of the law existing there; their obligation is chiefly of a negative character. Before an ecclesiastical superior can oblige a transient to the observance of a penalty attached to a law, or before he could proceed against one transgressing a law, it is necessary that the transgression be such as will disturb the public order; to contend that the observance of a law will bring a positive good to the community will not suffice as a basis for action. The existence and validity of this obligation on the part of the transient to avoid doing harm is derived from the natural law itself, for that law binds one always and everywhere to avoid scandal and to abstain from the infliction of harm. If such laws are violated by a positive act, the duty to remove the scandal or repair the harm done will naturally arise.[87]

When legislating for clerics who are transients in a certain territory, the legislator must distinguish carefully between matters

---

[85] Augustine, *Commentary,* I, 92; Blat, *Commentarium,* I, 90; Cappello, *De Censuris,* n. 19; idem, *Summa Iuris Canonici,* I, n. 80; Chelodi, *Ius Poenale,* n. 26; Claeys Bouuaert-Simenon, *Manuale Iuris Canonici* (4. ed., Gandae et Leodii, 1934), I, n. 164; Coronata, *Institutiones,* IV, n. 1712; De Meester, *Compendium,* III, n. 1713; Michiels, *Normae Generales,* pp. 317-324; Noldin-Schmitt, *Summa Theol. Moral.,* I, n. 152; Sole, *De Delictis et Poenis,* n. 106; Van Hove, *De Legibus,* n. 217; Vermeersch-Creusen, *Epitome,* I, n. 110; Wernz, *Ius Decretalium,* I, n. 107; VI, n. 151; Wernz-Vidal, *Ius Canonicum,* I, nn. 151, 156; VII, n. 228; Teodori, "Peregrini Quoad Censuras,"—*Apollinaris,* IV (1931), 139-141; Van Hove, "Leges Quae Ordini Publico Consulunt,"—*Ephemerides Theologicae Lovanienses,* I (1924), 156.

[86] *Loc. cit.*

[87] Van Hove, "Leges quae ordini publico consulunt,"—*ETL,* I (1924), 160.

that are concerned primarily with the good of the diocesan clerics and those which concern public order. Without a doubt there can be certain laws which may not be violated without giving scandal to the inhabitants of a diocese, and if this results, then certainly the ecclesiastical superior has the right to impose definite sanctions. Just which laws would be placed in this category must be determined in individual cases according to the peculiar circumstances in particular territories. Evidently the legislation of canons 132 and 133 has been established to protect the clerical state, not merely to further the sanctity of individual members thereof; the same can be said of those things which the common law considers unbecoming and alien to the clerical state.[38] Matters mentioned in canon 140, for instance, can be the source of scandal in a particular territory; if this be so, it is not beyond the power of the ordinary to legislate in such a manner as to make compliance by transients obligatory.[39] Can it then be said that even in the absence of scandal transient clerics may be bound by every law in a diocese that deals with the clerical state? This does not necessarily follow, for sometimes in making diocesan laws for clerics the bishop's purpose is to further their sanctity and to instill in the minds and hearts of the faithful greater reverence for them.[40]

---

[38] Canons 138, 139.

[39] The recommendation of the Sacred Consistorial Congregation of the 1st of July 1926 makes this evident:

a) Ordinarii locorum, quo sacerdotes valetudinis causa se conferre solent, sacerdotibus inibi commorantibus sedulo attenteque invigilent, vel per se vel per sacerdotes, quibus hoc peculiare munus demandaverint; et ad sacra facienda eos non admittant, nisi iis, quae supra diximus, praescriptis obtemperaverint.

b) Ut autem hi sacerdotes facilius in officio contineantur, opportunas poenas constituant quibus afficientur si scandalum dederint, vel si quoquo modo aliquod egerint, quod sacerdotali munere indignum sit.

c) Comminari etiam possunt suspensionem ipso facto incurrendam si publica theatra, cinematographa, ludos saltatorios deteraque huiusmodi profana spectacula adeant, vel si talarem vestem deponant.—*AAS*, XVIII (1926), 313.

[40] Cappello, *De Censuris*, n. 19; idem, *Summa Iuris Canonici*, I, n. 80; Michiels, *Normae Generales*, 321; Van Hove "Leges quae ordini publico

Whether or not a law is concerned with the public order must be judged from the interpretation of the ecclesiastical superior, at least when it is not clearly established that a particular statute has for its object the maintenance of the public order. He is the interpreter of the character of his law. In case of doubt subjects must accept his interpretation. It will be more advantageous, however, for the legislator to declare expressly that a particular law binds even transients. Ordinarily laws so enacted establish the presumption that they are concerned with the maintenance of the public order; it is presumed that the lawgiver included them under his law precisely for this public reason.[41]

ARTICLE III. EXEMPT RELIGIOUS

Canon 615 states that regulars, both men and women, except those nuns who are not subject to regular superiors, together with their houses and churches, are exempt from the jurisdiction of the local ordinary, except in such cases wherein the law has made express mention to the contrary. All orders of men with solemn vows are therefore included in this category, although it may be that not all the members are solemnly professed. Thus the novices, lay brothers and clerics with simple vows would enjoy the same exemption.[42] Among the nuns there may be communities which follow the rule of a male commmunity having solemn vows, but which are in no way subject to the superiors of that community. In such an instance the nuns do not enjoy exemption, but remain immediately subject to the local ordinary.[43] This exemption is not extended to institutes of simple vows, unless it has been conceded specially to them;[44] such a special concession,

---

consulunt,"—*ETL*, I (1924), 161; Teodori, "Peregrini Quoad Censuras,"—*Apollinaris*, IV (1931), 139-141.

[41] Michiels, *Normae Generales*, 322; Vermeersch-Creusen, *Epitome*, I, n. 110; Van Hove, *ETL*, I (1924), 167.

[42] Augustine, *Commentary*, III, 336; Schaefer, *De Religiosis*, 83.

[43] Fanfani, *De Iure Religiosorum ad Normam Codicis Iuris Canonici* (Taurini, 1925), n. 352.

[44] Canon 618.

for instance, has *de facto* been made to the Redemptorists[45] and Passionists.[46]

Even though a religious congregation have pontifical approval,[47] it does not enjoy the privilege of exemption in view of the common law. If such exemption from the coercive jurisdiction of the ecclesiastical superior is claimed, the burden of proof rests upon those claiming it, because without such an indult no congregation now enjoys the privilege.[48] Although the coercive powers of the local ordinary must be upheld in regard to congregations of pontifical approval, such communities enjoy full liberty in matters of internal government, for this is granted by the Code itself.[49] Institutes of diocesan right remain fully subject to the jurisdiction of the ordinary, and enjoy such independence only as the common law of the Code explicitly grants.[50]

This exemption being something personal, regulars and specially privileged clerics are withdrawn from the jurisdiction of the local ordinary everywhere and in all matters, even penal; they are not bound nor subject to penal measures imposed by a local ordinary for certain delicts, but may be bound in those matters in which their exemption privilege does not apply.[51] This exemption from the jurisdiction of the local ordinary or any consequent and immediate subjection to the Roman Pontiff[52] does not warrant the commission of crimes with impunity, for it is the duty of the re-

---

[45] Bull of Pius VI, *"Sacrosanctum,"* 21 aug. 1789—*Bullarii Romani Continuatio,* VI, Pars III, p. 2111; S. C. Ep. et Reg., *Congregationis SS. Redemptoris Super Privilegium,* 16 sept. 1864—*ASS,* I, 91-99.

[46] Bull of Clement XIV, *"Supremi Apostolatus,"* 16 dec. 1769—*Bullarii Romani Continuatio,* IV, 73; idem., *"Salvatoris Domini,"* 15 nov. 1769—*Bullarii Romani Continuatio,* IV, 105.

[47] Can. 488, 3o: Religionis iuris pontificii, religio quae vel approbationem vel saltem laudis decretum ab Apostolica Sede est consecuta.

[48] Augustine, *Commentary,* III, 336.

[49] Canon 618, § 2, n. 2.

[50] Canon 492, § 2.

[51] Claeys Bouuaert-Simenon, *Manuale Iuris Canonici,* I, n. 676; Cappello, *De Censuris,* n. 21. Instances in which exemption does not apply will be cited below.

[52] Noldin-Schmitt, *Summa Theol. Mor.,* I, n. 151.

ligious superior to uphold properly the penal sanctions of the common law.

At times it may happen that abuses exist in the house or churches of exempt religious; in such an instance, even though no scandal to the faithful developed as a result,[53] the bishop shall first warn the superiors to correct the wrong, and if they are negligent in correcting the abuse, the ordinary of the place is commanded to refer the matter to the Holy See.[54] In accordance with canon 617 this is the extent to which the local ordinary may proceed in this instance; he may not inflict any penal measures.[55] A single transgression of ecclesiastical law by a religious, or even by a number of religious, would not constitute the basis for action on the part of the local ordinary; what is required is a habitual and grave non-observance of the law.[56]

In the case of small houses (domus non formatae) in which there are less than six professed religious—or, if it is a clerical institute, less than four priests[57]—the Code grants the local ordinary a special surveillance though the house continues to enjoy exemption;[58] this surveillance does not partake of the nature of the surveillance of canon 2311. If in these houses there exist abuses which are the source of scandal to the faithful, the bishop is empowered to act provisionally to stop the scandal (*interim providere*),[59] that is, until the competent religious superior or the Holy See makes proper provision.[60] Unlike the case of a *domus*

[53] Coronata, *Institutiones,* I, n. 624, p. 828; Melo, *De Exemptione Regularium* (The Catholic University of America, Canon Law Studies, n. 12, Washington, D. C.: The Catholic University of America, 1921), p. 136.

[54] Canon 617, § 1.

[55] Coronata, *Institutiones,* I, p. 828, n. 624; Schaefer, *De Religiosis,* p. 474.

[56] Melo, *De Exemptione,* p. 137 quoting Bondini, *De Privilegio Exemptionis* (Romae, 1919), p. 66; Kramer, "An ius visitandi domus vel saltem ecclesias Regularium Ordinarii loci competat,"—*CpR,* IX (1928), 247; Schaefer, *De Religiosis,* p. 795.

[57] Canon 488, n. 5.

[58] Blat, *Commentarium,* Lib. II, Partes II-III (1938), n. 579: Coronata, *Institutiones,* I, p. 828, n. 624; Woywod, *A Practical Commentary on the Code of Canon Law* (4. ed., 2 vols., New York: Wagner, 1932), I, 267.

[59] Canon 617, § 2.

[60] Blat, *Commentarium,* Lib. II, Partes II-III, n. 146; Coronata, *Institutiones,* I, p. 828, n. 624; Melo, *De Exemptione,* p. 137; Toso, *Commentaria*

formata, the local ordinary need not warn the religious superior before he takes the action permitted by this canon.[61] Coronata[62] and Schaefer[63] contend that in virtue of this canon the ordinary is not permitted to use penal measures, but is permitted to provide for the needs of the occasion through administrative decrees only. Claeys Bouuaert-Simenon[64] and Toso,[65] on the other hand, hold that when scandal is present the bishop may indeed make use of administrative decrees, but should these prove ineffectual, he may also proceed to penalties. The reason given is that in such an instance the privilege of personal exemption has ceased. This latter opinion is more plausible, for it is the local ordinary's duty to provide for the removal of scandal, and if coercive measures are necessary to effect this, then it must be his right to use them.

If an exempt religious commits a delict when absent from his convent, the local ordinary has definitely assigned coercive powers. When such a religious is legitimately absent, although he may have returned to his convent, the local ordinary may proceed to the infliction of penal measures only after the proper superior has been notified.[66] Under the old law it was required that the delict which was committed had to be notorious and had to give rise to scandal among the people.[67] Although the New Code does not expressly demand this, yet one may assume the same conditions to be prerequired, for the deprivation of a privilege—in this instance exemption from the jurisdiction of the local ordinary—should be effected for a just cause only.[68] Only one

---

Minora, Lib. II, Pars II, p. 204; Vermeersch-Creusen, *Epitome,* I, n. 777; Kramer, "An ius visitandi . . . ,"—*CpR,* IX (1928), 247.

[61] Pruemmer, *Manuale Iuris Canonici* (4. et 5. ed., Friburgi Brisgoviae, 1927), p. 314, q. 240; Schaefer, *De Religiosis,* p. 474; Goyeneche, "Consultationes,"—*CpR,* IV (1930), 221.

[62] *Institutiones,* I, p. 828, n. 624.

[63] *De Religiosis,* p. 796.

[64] *Manuale Iuris Canonici,* I, n. 674.

[65] *Commentaria Minora,* Lib. II, Pars II, p. 204.

[66] Canon 616, § 2.

[67] Piatus Montensis, *Praelectiones Iuris Regularis* (3. ed., 2 vols., Tornaci [?]), II, 72-73.

[68] Augustine, *Commentary,* III, 340; Coronata, *Institutiones,* I, 827.

notification of the religious superior is required.[69] The local ordinary may not immediately proceed to the infliction of penalties, whether judicially or extra-judicially, yet he may gather such evidence of the commission of the crime as the circumstances permit and forward these to the religious superior.[70] How long the bishop should wait before considering the superior negligent and therefore consider himself justified in proceeding to the punishment of the delinquent is difficult to state with precision. Augustine[71] sets a period of fifteen days, while Coronata[72] sets twenty or thirty days. The nature of the delict committed and also the Constitutions of the institute concerned, may necessitate a certain length of time to proceed properly, which duration of time may be either more, or less, than the figures stated.[73] Briefly, then, it may be said that the ordinary should consider the circumstances involved in each case and allow that period of time which he feels is required to enable the religious superior to act justly. When the superiors have acted in the case, whether judicially or extra-judicially, they are to notify the local ordinary.[74] Should the religious superiors fail to punish the delinquent within the time allotted, the ordinary may proceed to impose whatever measures he deems proper, without giving new warnings.

In the event that an exempt religious is illegitimately absent from his convent, he is deprived of his privilege of exemption, and in case a delict is committed, the local ordinary may proceed to the infliction of proper penalties directly and immediately.[75] Among those *illegitimately* absent there must certainly be classed all fugitives—those who, without the permission of their superiors, desert the religious house with the intention of returning—,[76] and apostates—those who, having made profession of perpetual

---

[69] Coronata, *loc. cit.;* Piat, *Praelectiones,* II, 73.

[70] Piat, *Praelectiones,* II, 77-78.

[71] *Commentary,* III, 340.

[72] *Institutiones,* I, 827.

[73] Piat, *Praelectiones,* II, 78.

[74] Augustine, *Commentry,* III, 340; Coronata, *Institutiones,* I, 827; Piat, *Praelectiones,* II, 78.

[75] Canon 616, § 1.

[76] Canon 644, § 3.

vows, whether solemn or simple, unlawfully leave the religious house with the intention of not returning, or who, though they lawfully left the house, do not return.[77] Those expelled from an institute for a legitimate cause and in accordance with the Constitution are governed by this same legislation.[78] Canon 616, § 1, states that regulars unlawfully absent from their house, even under the pretext of having recourse to their superiors, do not enjoy the privilege of exemption. A religious who departs for this reason after being refused upon properly asking permission from an inferior superior, cannot be said to go "under pretext," for a pretext signifies a pretended or feigned reason; furthermore, religious are not denied the right to seek justice by going to a superior.[79] By the term *"domum"* there is meant a convent or monastery, the habitual domicile of a religious; this interpretation is according to the Council of Trent from which this law was taken.[80] Hence, as long as religious are illegitimately absent, though they may have banded together in a certain house, they cannot claim the privilege of exemption, for their abode would not be considered a religious house. Proper exception must be made if necessity forces religious from their houses, as in the case of war or persecution; unless the absence is unreasonably prolonged, such religious cannot be said to be illegitimately absent.[81]

How long a religious must be absent before a local ordinary can presume illegitimate absence, and thus feel justified to act, has not been determined in the Code. Vermeersch-Creusen state that such a one would not lose the privilege of exemption if he remains outside his house for one or even two days.[82] Augustine, however, citing a decretal of Pope Martin IV,[83] fixes an

[77] Canon 644, § 1.

[78] Bachofen, *Compendium Iuris Regularium* (New York: Benziger, 1903), 355; Santi, *Praelectiones,* III, tit. XXXI, n. 41, p. 292.

[79] Augustine, *Commentary,* III, 339.

[80] Sess. VI, *de ref.,* c. 3; sess. XXV, *de regularibus,* c. 4.

[81] Sacra Romana Rota, II Mechoacan, "Crediti"—*AAS,* III (1911), 432; cf. Claeys Bouuaert-Simenon, *Manuale Iuris Canonici,* I, n. 674; Melo, *De Exemptione,* p. 82; Pruemmer, *Manuale Iuris Canonici,* n. 241.

[82] *Epitome,* I, n. 573.

[83] C. 1, *de regularibus et transeuntibus ad religionem,* III, 8, in Extravag. Com.; this decretal is cited in the footnotes of the Gasparri edition of the Code in connection with canon 616, § 1.

absence of fifteen days as the length of time before such a presumption is warranted.[84]

In canon 615, which grants exemption from the jurisdiction of the local ordinary, exception is made for the cases in which the law has made express mention to the contrary. Thus the local ordinary would possess the right to exercise penal jurisdiction: when there is an interference by the religious with the ordinary's right to pontificate and preach in exempt churches;[85] when they do not partake in the periodical conferences of the clergy as the law prescribes;[86] when they refuse submission and obedience to Vicars and Prefects Apostolic in those things in which the Code makes them subject;[87] when the laws concerning the subjection of religious pastors to local ordinaries are not observed, as, for example, the regulations concerning prolonged absence of a pastor from his parish;[88] when religious parochial vicars refuse to comply with the regulations of the local ordinary in regard to their legitimate removal;[89] when there is an interference with the rights of the local ordinary during the visitation of clerical congregations of pontifical approval, although these be exempt;[90] when the prescriptions of the local ordinary are not observed in regard to money received for parishes or missions;[91] when the notice of the approaching admission to the novitiate or to profession is not sent in spite of the local ordinary's demand;[92] when they refuse to correct abuses existent in cloisters subject to the vigilance of the local ordinary;[93] when they refuse to adapt themselves to the regulations of the local ordinary in the case in which divine services in exempt churches interfere

---

[84] *Commentary,* III, 340; cf. also Melo, *De Exemptione,* p. 83.

[85] Canons 337, § 1; 1343, § 1.

[86] Canon 131, § 3.

[87] Canons 295; 296; 297; 298; 307.

[88] Canons 451, § 1; 454, § 5; 465, §§ 4, 5; 630; 631, §§ 1, 2.

[89] Canons 471, § 3; 472, 1°; 467, § 4; 477, § 1.

[90] Canon 512, § 2, 2°.

[91] Canon 533, § 1, 4°.

[92] Canon 552, § 1.

[93] Canon 603, § 1.

with parochial duties;[94] when they refuse to comply with the enactments of the local ordinary concerning the ringing of bells, the recitation of public prayers and the "oratio imperata";[95] when they act in opposition to the rights of the local ordinary concerning the erection of third orders secular;[96] when there is interference with the ordinary's right to confirm even in exempt places;[97] when the prescriptions concerning the granting, to transient priests, of permission to celebrate Mass are transgressed;[98] when the law concerning the determination of manual stipends is violated;[99] when delegation for the hearing of confessions, whether of the laity or of religious, is not sought from the local ordinary;[100] when the law concerning the promulgation of new indulgences is broken;[101] when the rights of the ordinary concerning the consecration or blessing of exempt places in his territory are denied him;[102] when public oratories or churches are erected without seeking the proper permission;[103] when prayers and exercises of piety are conducted in opposition to the regulations enacted by the local ordinary;[104] when the safeguards for divine worship and for the integrity of morals as prescribed by the local ordinary are not observed;[105] when the rules made to govern Benediction of the Blessed Sacrament are deliberately ignored;[106] when unusual pictures and images are publicly exposed in churches;[107] when relics without the proper authentication are exposed for veneration;[108] when public processions are conducted in defiance of the

[94] Canon 609, § 3.
[95] Canon 612.
[96] Canon 703, §§ 2, 3.
[97] Canon 792.
[98] Canon 804, § 3.
[99] Canon 831, § 3.
[100] Canons 874, § 1; 876.
[101] Canon 919, § 1.
[102] Canons 1155, § 1; 1157; 1169.
[103] Canon 1162, § 1.
[104] Canon 1259, § 1.
[105] Canon 1261, § 2.
[106] Canon 1274, § 1.
[107] Canon 1279, § 1.
[108] Canon 1283, § 1.

decrees of the local ordinary;[109] when a stipend, greater than that permitted by the bishop, is demanded for expenses in the celebration of Holy Mass;[110] when a reasonable request of the local ordinary concerning assistance in matters of catechetical and religious instruction is refused;[111] when preaching is undertaken without a previous request for the proper authorization or when the prescriptions of the local ordinary concerning preaching are ignored;[112] when legitimate contributions for the diocesan seminary are withheld, as also for other extraordinary diocesan assessments;[113] when the rights of the ordinary in the visitation of schools, asylums, hospitals and orphanages in matters of religious and moral instruction are denied;[114] when the laws governing the publication of books, etc. are not observed;[115] when they refuse to make a profession of faith as required by the Code;[116] when they deny the competency of the local ordinary in controversies for which the Code declares the ordinary competent.[117]

According to a private response, which, because of the general manner in which the questions were asked, has the force of a general interpretation, a local ordinary cannot make a quinquennial visitation of non-parochial churches that belong to regulars or others similarly exempt, merely to ensure the observance of the general laws of the Church. If he has legislated for his diocese in regard to matters of divine worship or the integrity of morals, he may make a visitation of these churches only when he has positive knowledge that his laws are not being observed.[118]

---

[109] Canons 1291, 1292.

[110] Canon 1303, § 3.

[111] Canons 1334, 1336.

[112] Canons 1338, §§ 2, 3; 1345.

[113] Canons 1355, 1356, 1505.

[114] Canons 1382, 1491.

[115] Canons 1385, § 2, 1386, 1388.

[116] Canon 1406 § 1, 7o.

[117] Canon 1579.

[118] Wernz-Vidal state the case which occasioned the response. They say, that in a certain city a delegate of the local ordinary made a canonical visitation of a Jesuit non-parochial church. The Jesuit provincial upon learning of this violation of exemption reminded the local ordinary that the church in question enjoyed exemption and consequently was not sub-

Being subject to the local ordinary in those things which are expressly singled out in the Code, religious, though they be otherwise exempt, become liable to penal measures which the local ordinary may impose.[119] Naturally, since these matters are under his jurisdiction, the ordinary has a right to legislate thereon, and as a result he has a right to add sanctions for the violation of his laws.[120] In general, however, exempt religious are not considered bound by the penalties established in a law of the local ordinary, even when this law is enacted concerning matters in which they are subject to him, unless this fact is expressly stated.[121] This same necessity of explicit declaration cannot be applied to non-exempt congregations. For them the simple rule of the canon applies: In all matters in which religious are subject to the local ordinary, he may coerce them even by penalties.[122] If the sanction threatened by the local ordinary for the violation of a certain law is a censure, then such exempt religious as Mendicants[123] and others who enjoy this same privilege, as the

---

ject to the quinquennial visitation of the Ordinary or his delegate. The local ordinary repudiated the provincial's plea and denied the claim of exemption.—*Ius Canonicum,* III, 429-430 in footnote. The litigated question was thereupon forwarded to the Holy See in the following queries:

"I. Utrum ordinarius loci templa Societatis Jesu in sua diocesi existentia modo praedicto quinto quoque anno visitare possit? Et quatenus negative:

"II. Utrum in casu, quo leges diocesanae non quidem novam materiam juxta canonem 1261 afferunt, sed solum leges ecclesiasticas urget ordinarius ad visitationem manum apponere possit? Et quatenus negative:

"III. Utrum visitatio, de qua in canone 1261, § 2, extendi possunt responsa S. C. Ep. et Reg. ante novum codicem data, ut nempe ordinarius visitationis jure in tantum solum generatim utitur, in quantum positivam habeat notitiam leges particulares a se latas in ecclesiis regularium exemptorum non observari? Responsum datum die 8 mensis Aprilis, 1924: ad Ium, IIum, et IIIum, negative; ad IVum affirmative."—*Commentarium pro Religiosis,* IX (1928), 243-247.

[119] Canons 619; 2226, § 1.

[120] Canon 2220, § 1.

[121] Cappello, *De Censuris,* n. 24; Claeys Bouuaert-Simenon, *Manuale Iuris Canonici,* I, n. 676; Coronata, *Institutiones,* I, 810.

[122] Coronata, *Institutiones,* I, 811; Vermeersch-Creusen, *Epitome,* I, n. 779.

[123] Bull of Sixtus IV, *"Regimini universalis,"* 31 aug. 1474—*Bullarium Diplomatum et Privilegiorum Romanorum Pontificum,* V, 217; St. Alphonsus, *Theologia Moralis* (Matriti, 1876), VII, n. 26; Mocchegiani, *Iuris-*

Jesuits,[124] would not be liable thereto. This special privilege of exemption has its application, however, only with reference to threatened censures, and not with reference to threatened vindictive penalties or penal remedies. Nevertheless there are three cases in which these religious become liable even to censures at the hand of the local ordinary. These cases are: 1) preaching without the bishop's permission; 2) hearing confessions without his authorized jurisdiction; 3) setting up images of an unusual and offensive character for public veneration.[125]

---

prudentia Ecclesiastica ad Usum et Commoditatem utriusque Cleri (3 vols., Quaracchi, 1904), III, nn. 801-804.

[124] Bull of Paul III, "*Licet Debitum,*" 18 oct. 1549—*Bullarium Diplomatum et Privilegiorum Romanorum Pontificum,* VI, 394.

[125] Gregory XV, const. "*Inscrutabili,*" 5 feb. 1622—*Fontes,* n. 199.

CHAPTER VIII

The Reservation of Penalties

The reservation of penalties is a matter whose consideration will always be linked more closely with the factor of their remission than with that of their infliction. Nevertheless, in as far as the presence of any reservation cannot arise apart from a person's contracting of a penalty either as the result of the law's absolute disposition or as the effect of a superior's discretional intervention in any given case, it is naturally indicated at this point at least briefly to consider the question of reservation from this secondary angle. Since the inflicted penalty may disclose one or the other of two possible purposes, namely, a medicinal purpose in connection with censures and a legally vindictive aim in connection with other penalties, it is necessary to know in which of these two forms the penalty was contracted if one is also to know by which means it is later to be relaxed.

In the extrajudicial imposition of medicinal penal measures, there are two ways of effecting this: either by making a law having attached thereto a censure for its violation; or by direct action on the part of the superior by way of precept. If a law is enacted and the penalty is not an *ab homine* but a *latae sententiae* censure, then the reservation must be expressly stated; if this is not done, the censure is not reserved, for canon 2245, § 4, states that a *latae sententiae* censure is not reserved unless this is expressly stated in the law. The second method of imposing a censure is by direct action of the superior. Here again distinctions are in order. It is possible for the superior either to apply the penalty here and now, or so to word his precept as to make a second act necessary on his part, or, finally, to issue a precept that implies the incurring of a censure *ipso facto* for the commission or omission of a certain act.

Exemplification, perhaps, will help to make these distinctions more clear. A superior may suspend a cleric immediately in view of the act he has committed and the great scandal that has resulted; such a censure is imposed *ab homine*[1] for its absolution is reserved to the superior inflicting it.[2] Again, a bishop may summon a priest and declare: "If you do that again, I shall suspend you"; then, upon the commission of the forbidden act the bishop concerned may proceed to the infliction of the censure threatened; such a penalty is also imposed *ab homine,* and therefore its absolution is reserved to the bishop who has inflicted the penalty. Finally, a bishop may declare to one of his subjects: "If you do that again, you will be *ipso facto* suspended." The problem is in connection with this third example; as the result of such a declaration, is the censure to be considered as imposed *ab homine,* and if so, has the bishop reserved its absolution to himself by the words used?[3]

The difficulty spoken of becomes evident when one tries to harmonize the various canons. Canon 2217, § 1, n. 3, states that an *ab homine* censure is one that is inflicted either by way of precept or by a condemnatory sentence; canon 2245, § 2, states that an *ab homine* censure is reserved to him who inflicted the censure or issued the sentence, while § 4 of the same canon states that a *latae sententiae* censure is not reserved unless this is explicitly stated. If, in the last example given—a precept forbidding an act and determining a censure to be incurred *ipso facto* for its violation—the censure is imposed *ab homine,* then the bishop need not express words denoting its reservation, for this effect would automatically follow from the *ab homine* character of the penalty; if the penalty is not imposed *ab homine,* then its reservation is not effected without an express statement to that effect when the precept was given. If one holds that every precept implies an *ab homine* intervention, how can this be reconciled with § 4 of canon 2245, for the censure now discussed was incurred *ipso facto* without further action on the

[1] Canon 2217, § 1, n. 3.

[2] Canon 2245, § 2.

[3] For a complete and detailed consideration of this problem see: Moriarity, *The Extraordinary Absolution from Censures* (The Catholic University of America, Canon Law Studies, n. 113; Washington, D. C.: The Catholic University of America, 1938), pp. 91-108.

part of a superior, and § 4 says that a *latae sententiae* censure is not reserved?

Most canonists[4] admit the existence of a *latae sententiae ab homine* censure—the *latae sententiae* censure attached to a particular precept. Michiels[5] considers this censure as being imposed neither *ab homine* nor *a iure* exclusively, but *"tamquam a iure,"* while Roberti[6] calls it a censure imposed *"per praeceptum ad instar legis."* The solutions of the canonists vary. It will therefore be profitable to consider the outstanding opinions before a conclusion is reached.

Creusen[7] offers one solution, which several authors accepted after him.[8] He considers the word *praecepto* of canon 2245, § 4, as referring to a general precept. The old law, he contends, distinguished between the particular precept administered to an individual and the general precept given to a community; further, in the old law an *ab homine* censure, namely, one imposed by particular precept either as a *latae* or *ferendae sententiae* censure, was always considered reserved. Although admitting that the Code nowhere makes an explicit distinction between a general and a particular precept, he says that this distinction is implied, for without it one cannot explain canon 2245, nor canons 2247, 2252 and 2253.[9] But, despite this apparently plausible reasoning of Creusen, it must still be admitted that his interpretation does not obviate the crux of the problem. For, since the Code simply

---

[4] Ayrinhac-Lydon, *Penal Legislation*, n. 35; Cipollini, *De Censuris*, p. 7; Coronata, *Institutiones*, IV, 78; De Meester, *Compendium*, III, Pars II, pp. 141, 169; Salucci, *Diritto Penale*, I, 198, nota 1; Sole, *De Delictis et Poenis*, n. 70; Vermeersch-Creusen, *Epitome*, III, n. 406.

[5] "De reservatione censurae latae sententiae praecepto peculiari adnexae," *ETL*, IV (1927), 192.

[6] "An censura latae sententiae per praeceptum constituta sit reservata?"—*Apollinaris*, VI (1933), 342.

[7] "De Reservatione Censurae Praecepto Latae"—*Jus Pont.*, IV (1924), 26-29; *Epitome*, III, nn. 406, 443; "La reserve des censures 'ab homine,"—*NRT*, LV (1928), 436.

[8] Blat, *Commentarium*, Lib. V, p. 101; Cappello, *De Censuris*, n. 68; Cocchi, *Commentarium*, Lib. V, p. 108; De Meester, *Compendium*, III, Pars II, p. 170.

[9] *Epitome*, III, nn. 406, 443.

does not make this distinction, it is hardly justified to supply it on private initiative for the sole reason of solving an intricate question, in relation to which the use of any other means would appear less felicitous if it did not abstract from a primarily objective outlook or from a solidly juridical viewpoint. Furthermore, it seems difficult, if not impossible, to specify any canon in the Code which in any way lends confirmation to the statement of pre-Code authors who held every *latae* or *ferendae sententiae* penalty to be a reserved penalty if only it was inflicted *ab homine*.

Salucci[10] is opposed to the foregoing opinion, for he claims that it is incorrect to say that the term *praecepto* refers to general precepts only. He concludes from the passage "*censura latae sententiae . . . in lege vel praecepto*" that all *latae sententiae* censures are here considered, whether they be enacted *a iure* or imposed *ab homine*. He would limit § 2 of canon 2245 to *ferendae sententiae* censures exclusively. Because *latae sententiae* censures are more odious than *ferendae sententiae* censures, it is his contention that no *latae sententiae* censures are *per se* reserved, and that explicit reservation must be made if a superior intends its reservation. The objection to this opinion is that the Code simply says that a censure is reserved to him who inflicts it, without mentioning *ferendae sententiae* as a necessary qualification.[11]

Sole[12] attempts to simplify the solution by stating that the phrase *censura latae sententiae* in canon 2245, § 4, includes also the censure imposed or incurred *ab homine*. Hence, unless explicit mention of reservation is made either in the law or in the precept, one may consider the censure as non-reserved. This opinion, however, seems only partially to solve the difficulty, for it practically passes over the words *ab homine*, and makes censures incurred as a result of a precept equal to those enacted *a iure*. It thus fails to evaluate properly the fact that an *ab homine* imposed censure is reserved. Cappello, in an article in 1920,[13]

---

[10] *Diritto Penale*, I, 198-200 in nota.

[11] Coronata, *Institutiones*, IV, n. 1750.

[12] *De Delictis et Poenis*, n. 173, 2.

[13] "De absolutione a censuris 'ab homine' ac de metu relate ad censuras," *NRT*, XLVII (1920), 525-527.

seems to favor a similar solution. He states that a censure to be incurred without actual infliction is *per se* not reserved; if, however, the censure must be inflicted by special act of the superior, then it is reserved.

Finally, Michiels[14] and Roberti[15] offered the solution that a censure incurred *ipso facto* as the result of the violation of a precept is not to be considered *ab homine* but *"tamquam a iure"* and is therefore *per se* not reserved, in accordance with the provision of canon 2245, § 4. They further distinguished between a precept which is similar to a penal law, *praeceptum ad instar legis,* and which implies in the act of its violation that the penalty is incurred *ipso facto,* and a precept which corresponds to a condemnatory sentence, *praeceptum ad instar sententiae,* and which demands that the penalty is still to be inflicted. The conclusion drawn as a result of this distinction was that when a *latae sententiae* censure is threatened by a precept *ad instar legis,* so that it is incurred without a precept *ad instar sententiae,* it is not to be considered as imposed *ab homine* but *tamquam a iure.*

As a result of this consideration of the attempts to settle the apparent contradiction between § 2 and § 4 of canon 2245, only one conclusion can be reached: the reservation of the *latae sententiae ab homine* imposed censure is doubtful in law. Applying the principles enunciated in the Code itself, that in penalties the milder interpretation is to be applied,[16] and that in the case of doubt, either in relation to the law or in relation to a fact, the reservation does not take effect,[17] it can be said that a *latae sententiae ab homine* imposed censure is *per se* not reserved.[18] Hence, unless a superior, when administering a precept which threatens a *latae sententiae* censure, uses some phrase indicating the censure's reservation, the censure is not reserved to him for absolution. Thus, if a bishop were to say to one of his subjects: "Unless, within ten days, you retract what you wrote, you will

[14] "De reservatione censurae . . . ," *ETL,* IV (1927), 180-194, 613-619.

[15] "An censura latae sententiae . . . ," *Apollinaris,* VI (1933), 341-348.

[16] Canon 2219, § 1.

[17] Canon 2245, § 4.

[18] Coronata, *Institutiones,* IV, 163.

be automatically excommunicated," the censure incurred for the non-fulfillment of the precept would not be reserved, because reservation was not expressly stated in the precept. In order to reserve such a censure to himself, the superior would have to add the words: "this censure is reserved to me" or its equivalent. By doing so he would remove all doubts and be certain of the desired reservation.

One other question in regard to reservation now remains. What are the powers and rights which an inferior superior enjoys if he wishes to enact as particular legislation a penal law that already appears in the common law. Canon 2247, § 1, forbids ordinaries to attach to a delict another censure which is reserved to themselves if the Holy See has already attached to the same delict a censure which is reserved to itself. Just what does this imply? In the first place, a local ordinary may not add another censure, whether of the same kind[19] or of a different kind, and Holy See could not pronounce a second reserved excommunication in regard to canon 2320—the abuse of the Blessed Sacrament. Whether or not reservation in opposition to this canon would entail invalidity is disputed; the preponderance of opinion, however, favors the interpretation of the words *"censuram nequit ferre"* as implying invalidity.[21] This lower superior may add a censure of his own and of the same kind as long as it is *"nemini reservata"*; prudence would dissuade such action, however, for there would simply be a multiplication of penalties without any positive good being effected.[22] Since canon 2247, § 1, simply employs the phrase *aliam censuram,* it is evident that a lower authority may not attach any other censure whose absolution is reserved to itself for absolution. But an intermediate superior is within his right to attach a

---

[19] Augustine, *Commentary,* VIII, 134; Cappello, *De Censuris,* n. 69; Coronata, *Institutiones,* IV, n. 1751; Roberti, *De Delictis et Poenis,* nn. 286, 292.

reserve it to himself.[20] Thus a superior who is an inferior to the

[20] Augustine, *op. cit.,* VIII, 135; Coronata, *loc. cit.;* Roberti, *loc. cit.*

[21] Blat, *Commentarium,* Lib. V, p. 103; Coronata, *loc. cit.;* Salucci, *Diritto Penale,* p. 260; Woywod, *Commentary,* II, n. 2088; *contra,* Augustine, *Commentary,* VIII, 134.

[22] Augustine, *loc. cit.;* Cocchi, *Commentarium,* VIII, n. 112; Coronata, *loc. cit.*

vindictive penalty over and above the already extant censure which the Holy See has reserved to itself for absolution.[23]

If the common law has simply threatened a censure without reserving it to any particular superior, such a censure may be reserved by a bishop to himself, but if such an action is undertaken then there should exist particular circumstances to justify this specific application over and above the sanction provided by the common law. This stipulation harmonizes perfectly with the demand of canon 2246, which states that a censure should not be reserved unless the reservation is demanded by the peculiar gravity of the offense, the necessity of maintaining ecclesiastical discipline, and the need of correcting the morals of the faithful more effectively.[24] Should it happen that the Holy See through legislation which is subsequent to legislation enacted by a local ordinary attaches a particular censure to a certain delict and reserves it to itself, this Pontifical action automatically nullifies the reservation decreed by the local ordinary, for, by reserving the censure to itself, the Holy See withdraws the case from the jurisdiction of the lower superior.[25]

---

[23] Augustine, *loc. cit.;* cf. Coronata, *loc. cit.*

[24] Cappello, *De Censuris,* n. 69; Coronata, *Institutiones,* IV, n. 1751; Salucci, *Diritto Penale,* p. 260.

[25] Coronata, *loc. cit.;* Roberti, *De Delictis et Poenis,* n. 292.

CHAPTER IX

The Infliction of Coercive Measures

ARTICLE I. THE SUPERIOR

Every superior enjoying legislative power has the right to exercise coercive jurisdiction, whether in the enactment of laws or in the issuance of precepts.[1] This power he may exercise directly and immediately, or indirectly through another to whom he grants the required delegation.[2] Besides the possession of an office or of delegation which bestows such jurisdiction, it is also required that the superior be free from every legal disability which hinders the valid exercise of jurisdiction. Thus one possessing ordinary jurisdiction must be free from every suspension or excommunication imposed by means of a declaratory or condemnatory sentence,[3] while one who has been delegated, as, for instance, the Vicar General, must be sure that delegation has not been recalled, and that the superior delegating him did not lose his own jurisdiction.[4]

It is certainly true that within his territory a superior may exercise his jurisdiction to the fullest extent. Outside his territory he may also exercise extrajudicial coercive jurisdiction upon those subject to him, whether these be within or outside of his own territory.[5] If an abuse or delict is notorious, no judicial procedure is required to establish its certainty, for such a trial has for its purpose the determination of guilt. Thus, for example, in order to secure the avoidance of future crimes, an ecclesiastical superior is permitted to inflict a suspension on a subject of his by

---

[1] Canon 2220, § 1. Cf. Chapter VI for an enumeration of the superiors having this power.

[2] Canon 199, § 1.

[3] Canons 2264, 2285.

[4] Canon 319; Cappello, *De Censuris*, n. 30; Suarez, *De Censuris*, disp. II, sec. IV, n. 2; Wernz-Vidal, *Ius Canonicum*, VII, n. 236.

[5] The question of the subject of a superior's coercive jurisdiction has been considered in chapter VII.

means of a statute or precept, for such an act would not be the exercise of judicial jurisdiction in an alien territory, which is prohibited to a superior under ordinary circumstances.[6]

ARTICLE II. PENAL REMEDIES

Although the ecclesiastical superior possesses the power to inflict coercive measures, he must ever be mindful of his duty to prevent transgressions of the law and to eliminate disturbances of the established order whenever possible. The primary work of the Church, and therefore of superiors, is to seek the salvation and sanctification of its members, not their punishment. Accordingly, there is outlined in the Code a mode of procedure which is to be used in so far as the prudence of the superior and the circumstances of the case dictate.

The penal remedies suggested in the Code are preventive measures to avert the lapse into grave offenses. The very fact that they are called penal remedies, supposes that the conduct of the individual to whom they are to be applied is blameworthy, although evidence as to the commission of a delict may not be had.[7] Ordinarily the superior is advised, though not obliged, to try admonitions and salutary extrajudicial precepts, or even light corrective penances. This method may be employed when there is well-founded suspicion, or likely, though not certain, evidence of some delict, for full certitude is not necessary.[8] According to the different circumstances and needs of the individual cases, these remedies may take the form of advice and counsel, warning or caution.

The knowledge that the superior possesses as to the suspicion of, or proximate occasion of, the commission of an offense, may be obtained from various sources: from ecclesiastics or laics, or through immediate observation, as when making a visitation.[9]

---

[6] Canon 201, § 2. Cf. Vermeersch-Creusen, *Epitome*, I, n. 320; Cappello, *De Censuris*, n. 37.

[7] Chelodi, *Ius Poenale*, n. 54; Coronata, *Institutiones*, IV, n. 1842; De Meester, *Compendium*, III, Pars II, n. 1800; Woywod, *Commentary*, II, 462.

[8] Canon 2307.

[9] Instructio S. C. EE. et RR., 11 iun. 1880, Art. V—*Fontes*, n. 2005.

Naturally, the first obligation is to determine the truth of the information possessed. This is to be done simply and informally, in such a way as not to suggest a formal trial or to bring discredit upon the subject concerned.[10] Absolute certitude of the guilt, or even of the danger of the law's transgression, is not demanded before the superior may admonish one of his subjects; a well-founded suspicion will suffice.[11]

Justice demands that under ordinary conditions the delinquent be given a hearing in regard to the charges alleged against him. At such times the guilty may even be made acquainted with some of the evidence, although it is not advisable to make known the source of the information.[12] If the accused cannot prove innocence, then it will be proper for the superior or one appointed by him[13] to give a paternal admonition, appropriate instructions and corrections. The spirit of charity will advise the application of penances[14] rather than the immediate application of ecclesiastical penalties, especially when the superior wishes to avoid the scandal that may arise among the faithful if a penalty were imposed, or when he remits a penalty but feels that some penance should be done.[15]

If scandal or serious disorder has arisen as a result of an individual's act, the ordinary, either personally or through a delegate, may issue a stern rebuke (*correptio*) to the delinquent.[16] It differs from the preceding paternal admonition inasmuch as the rebuke is administered when scandal or disorder has arisen.[17] This rebuke is still a mere corrective measure; however severe it

---

[10] Droste-Messmer, *Canonical Procedure in Disciplinary and Criminal Cases of Clerics* (New York, 1887), p. 147; Vermeersch-Creusen, *Epitome,* III, n. 503.

[11] Ayrinhac-Lydon, *Penal Legislation,* n. 180; Coronata, *Institutiones,* IV, n. 1842.

[12] Droste-Messmer, *Canonical Procedure,* p. 148.

[13] Not the Vicar General, unless he has a special mandate—Canon 2220, § 2; cf. Augustine, *Commentary,* VIII, 268; Coronata, *Institutiones,* IV, n. 1841.

[14] Canon 2312-2313.

[15] Coronata, "Pene e Procedimenti ad Modum Praecepti,"—*Perfice Munus,* VII (1932), 270.

[16] Canon 2308.

[17] Coronata, *Institutiones,* IV, n. 1843.

may be, it should not contain any threat of punishment properly so called, for if this were the case, it would partake of the nature of the precept.[18]

Both the paternal admonition as well as the more severe rebuke may be made privately or publicly. If made in public, it should take place in the presence of the chancellor or notary, or before two witnesses; it may also be given by letter.[19] In the latter instance care must be taken that a record of proper delivery and reception is kept. Whether the admonition or rebuke (or both) was private or public, it should be recorded; if secret, in the secret archives;[20] if public, in the public records. A record of the exact words is not required; it will suffice if a mere notation of the administration of the admonition or rebuke is made, with a notation whether this was given once or more frequently.[21] The formalities observed in the proceeding are to make it impressive as also to furnish proof of obstinacy;[22] they are intended for the correction of the delinquent by calling his attention to his questionable conduct, and to furnish a definite foundation for the application of ecclesiastical penalties.

The Code does not prescribe any exact form in which the secret admonitions are to be given, while in the event of public admonitions it simply states that they should be made before the notary, before witnesses, or by means of a letter properly dispatched. It is left to the prudent judgment of the superior which form is to be used. So also is the repetition of these admonitions left to the decision of the superior, for the Code simply states *semel vel pluries.*[23]

---

[18] Coronata, *Institutiones,* IV, n. 1841; Vermeersch-Creusen, *Epitome,* III, n. 503.

[19] Canons 2309, § 2; 2143; De Meester, *Compendium,* III, Pars II, n. 1804 nota 1.

[20] Canon 2309, § 5.

[21] Instructio S. C. EE. et RR., 11 iun. 1880, Art. VI—*Fontes,* n. 2005.

[22] Cappello, *De Censuris,* n. 34, 5º; Droste-Messmer, *Canonical Procedure,* p. 151; Roberti, *De Delictis et Poenis,* n. 283; Vermeersch-Creusen, *Epitome,* III, n. 503.

[23] Canon 2309, § 6. De Meester implies that one warning is sufficient in all cases in which the law does not expressly call for repeated admonitions.—*Compendium,* III, Pars II, n. 1724.

Under the old law, three admonitions were required with an interval of two days, or at least one peremptory decree.[24] This regulation no longer exists under the new Code.[25]

If there is question of inflicting a censure *ferendae sententiae* censure threatened in the law, one admonition is sufficient. The law may contain a general threat of punishment against future delinquents, but the punishment is inflicted only in particular cases by the superior. Whether or not a canonical warning is necessary for the valid infliction of such a censure is disputed. Some authors hold that such an infliction would probably be invalid;[26] others, however, do not consider it invalid, but unjust.[27] In canon 2233, § 2, it is prescribed that a warning be issued before a censure is inflicted as a *ferendae sententiae* penalty, for the sake of determining the presence of contumacy. No such warning is demanded for the incurring of a *latae sententiae* censure, for the morally imputable violation of a sanctioned law is sufficient to incur these censures; the law itself is a sufficient warning, and the knowledge of the law and sanction serves as the canonical *monitio,* without the necessity of canonical admonitions in the strict sense of the word. In prescribing the admonition, however, the canon presents no evidence that the warning is necessary for validity. Consequently, in view of canon 11, which demands the inclusion of an invalidating clause in the law in order to connote the corresponding effect of invalidity, it is safe to maintain that because of the *dubium iuris* this warning need not be regarded as a condition necessary for validity.

---

[24] Cappello, *De Censuris,* n. 34; Chelodi, *Ius Poenale,* n. 28; Kober, *Kirchenbann,* 145-156; Santi-Leitner, *Praelectiones Juris Canonici* (2 vols., Ratisbonae, 1898), I, n. 51; Wernz, *Ius Decretalium,* VI, n. 167.

[25] Coronata, *Institutiones,* IV, n. 1724.

[26] Cappello, *De Censuris,* n. 34; Roberti, *De Delictis et Poenis,* n. 283; Salucci, *Diritto Penale,* I, 160; Sole, *De Delictis et Poenis,* n. 132.

[27] Augustine, *Commentary,* VIII, 117; Claeys Bouuaert-Simenon, *Manuale Iuris Canonici,* III, n. 529; De Meester, *Compendium,* III, Pars II, n. 1724; Suarez, *De Remotione Parochorum Aliisque Processibus Tertiae Partis Lib. IV Cod. Iur. Can.* (Romae, 1931), p. 231, 4.

ARTICLE III. THE PRECEPT

When the superior is informed of some serious faults or dangerous occasions existing among his subjects, and has found admonitions and rebukes ineffective, or when he positively knows that admonitions will be disregarded, he may immediately proceed to the issuance of the canonical precept. Therein he will give a special command to the delinquent, pointing out what must be done or avoided in the future, sanctioning that command with the threat of a certain and clearly determined punishment.[28] Quite naturally the greatest precaution is required, even when a summary investigation has revealed sufficient grounds for action.[29]

How the superior will proceed in issuing a canonical precept can be fundamentally determined from canons 24 and 2225 together with Article VIII of the Instruction of 1880.[30] He will first cite the delinquent to appear at a stated time to hear the injunction. Such an occasion will give the accused the opportunity to offer a defense if such be possible. If he appears, then the command of the superior, the cause of the precept[31] as well as the threatened penalty may be read to him in the presence of two witnesses, whether ecclesiastics or laics. These witnesses must be such as are worthy of credence and who fulfill the requirements of law,[32] so that, if necessary, they may be called upon in court to bear witness to the issuance of the precept. Possessing the canonical requisites, such witnesses can then not be rejected as unfit, suspected or disqualified.[33] The record of the transaction should be signed by the parties present, also by the delinquent himself,

---

[28] Canon 2310; Instructio S. C. EE. et RR., 11 iun. 1880, Art. VII—*Fontes*, n. 2005. As to the imposition of a censure *per modum praecepti*, the limits within which this is possible will be discussed in Art. IV of this chapter.

[29] Lega, *Praelectiones in Textum Iuris Canonici de Iudiciis Ecclesiasticis* (4 vols., Romae, 1896-1901), IV, 288.

[30] For the precept in the case of a suspension "ex informata conscientia" see canon 2193; also, Murphy, *Suspension Ex Informata Conscientia*, pp. 99-104.

[31] Ayrinhac-Lydon, *Penal Legislation*, n. 44.

[32] Canons 1756-1758.

[33] Michiels, *Normae Generales*, I, 517; Toso, *Commentaria Minora*, I, 73.

although he is not obliged to do so. This record is then filed in the archives.

The precept should be drawn up in writing, containing the name of the superior issuing it, the name of the guilty party, the precept or command as to what must be done or avoided, and finally the sanction—the punishment that will be inflicted if the command is not obeyed. If the penalty to be incurred is vindictive, the time during which it will be in force must also be stated.

Instead of the oral announcement of the precept in the presence of witnesses, there may also be employed an intimation that is made in writing, that is, by means of a legal document. Just what constitutes a "legal document" when there is question of a precept is nowhere stated in the Code. Although in certain canonical procedures, special forms of precepts are spoken of (e.g., citation), these have no application to canon 24.[84] There is no definite formula or any particular wording prescribed for validity.[85] It may therefore be said that any decree of a superior which contains the facts pertinent to the precept—the name of the delinquent, the delict or offense attributed to him, the command of the superior, and the punishment threatened—subscribed by the superior and a notary, with proper notation of the place, day, month and year, can be considered a "legal document" in the sense of canon 24.[86] Woywod[87] and Coronata[88] contend that a private letter of a superior which contains the ordinary formalities (place, date, signature) and which clearly signifies the intention of the superior to impose a precept on a subject, could be called a "legal document," although not bearing the subscription of a notary. This seems to carry the meaning of the term too far; Coronata notes the weakness of this contention, for he adds that it would

[84] "Praecepta, singulis data, eos quibus dantur, ubique urgent, sed iudicialiter urgeri nequeunt et cessant resoluto iure praecipientis, nisi per legitimum documentum aut coram duobus testibus imposita fuerint."

[85] Wernz-Vidal, *Ius Canonicum,* n. 242.

[86] Michiels, *Normae Generales,* I, 517; Roberti, *De Delictis et Poenis,* n. 263; Van Hove, *De Legibus,* n. 363.

[87] *Commentary,* I, n. 18.

[88] *Institutiones,* I, n. 33, 6º.

be better that the ordinary have present a notary and have the seal affixed.[39]

The two methods outlined above are the *ordinary* (*ordinarie*) method of procedure; strict adherence thereto, however, is not required for the validity of the precept, as the very words of canon 2225 indicate.[40] It is possible for the superior to issue a precept by means of a private document delivered to the delinquent or also orally in his presence, but in the latter case especially it would be difficult to furnish any satisfactory proof of the imposition of the precept if the delinquent would interpose a recourse against it. Furthermore, even in the event that no recourse is interposed the precept could readily lack the continued duration that the superior may wish to attach to it.[41] Canon 24 explicitly states that precepts cease to bind with the expiration of the authority of the one who imposed them, unless they were given in the form of a legal document or before two witnesses. Therefore, even though a precept was given for a definite period of time, it would lose its binding force upon the death of the superior who imposed it, unless the prescriptions of the canon for its subsequent continuance were carried out.[42] If the precept was given in a manner other than the methods mentioned in the canon, it would not be invalid nor could it be ignored, although it would lose its force upon the demise of the superior. Hence, precepts given privately or informally by a superior are not invalid: they pertain to the extrajudicial forum to the same extent as those formally imposed, and would make one liable to the penalties threatened for nonobservance.[43]

Once a precept threatening a penalty has been imposed, no further admonition is required if that precept is violated. If the threatened penalty is a *latae sententiae* penalty it takes effect

---

[39] *Institutiones,* IV, n. 1711.

[40] Cappello, *De Censuris,* n. 32; Coronata, *Institutiones,* IV, n. 1711; Roberti, *De Delictis et Poenis,* n. 263; Salucci, *Diritto Penale,* p. 124.

[41] Cicognani, *Canon Law,* p. 639; D'Annibale, *Summula Theol. Mor.,* I, 329, nota 25.

[42] Michiels, *Normae Generales,* I, 517.

[43] Cicognani, *Canon Law,* p. 640; Coronata, *Institutiones,* IV, n. 1711; Maroto, *Institutiones,* I, n. 267; Michiels, *Normae Generales,* I, 518.

immediately;[44] if it is a *ferendae sententiae* penalty, the superior may proceed immediately to its infliction.[45] If, however, the delinquent recedes from his contumacy before the penalty is actually inflicted, a censure can no longer be imposed.[46] The reason for this is that a censure is a medicinal penalty inflicted upon a person for the purpose of breaking his contumacy which is a certain contempt of the censure or the authority of the one inflicting the censure.[47] Contempt for the natural law or even the positive divine law is not sufficient, but there must be a contempt for an ecclesiastical law to which a specific censure is attached.[48] Canon 2242, § 2, states that when there is question of *ferendae sententiae* censures, a person is considered contumacious when, notwithstanding warnings and admonitions, he does not desist from the offense, or refuses to do penance for the offense and to make due preparation for the damages and scandals caused thereby. If, therefore, a delinquent recedes from his contumacy either as soon as the cause of the precept is made known to him, or before a *ferendae sententiae* censure is imposed, he no longer is liable to the censure; the superior however may impose a vindictive penalty. If the superior does inflict a censure under such circumstances, the presumption is that in the superior's judgment contumacy has not yet ceased, and since it is his right to decide when the contumacy ceases, the censure is considered valid, at least in the external forum.[49]

---

[44] Canon 2242, § 2.

[45] *Pontificia Commissio ad Codicis Canones Authentice Interpretandos,* 14 iul. 1922: "Utrum, ad normam can. 2233, § 2, ob violationem praecepti peculiaris, quod comminatum erat censura ferendae sententiae, statim post delictum comprobatum censura infligi possit; an vero praemittenda sit nova monitio." Resp.: Affirmative ad Iam partem; negative ad 2am.—*AAS*, XIV (1922), 530. Cf. also Coronata, *Institutiones,* IV, n. 1724; Cocchi, *Commentarium,* VIII, n. 49; Wernz-Vidal, *Ius Canonicum,* VII, n. 244.

[46] Canon 2242, § 1: "Censura punitur tantummodo delictum . . . cum contumacia coniunctum"; cf. Vermeersch-Creusen, *Epitome,* III, n. 427.

[47] Cappello, *De Censuris,* n. 24; Coronata, *Institutiones,* IV, n. 1743; De Meester, *Compendium,* III, Pars II, n. 1732; Vermeersch-Creusen, *Epitome,* III, n. 438; Wernz, *Ius Decretalium,* VI, n. 145.

[48] Coronata, *loc. cit.;* Wernz, *op. cit.,* VI, n. 155.

[49] Augustine, *Commentary,* VIII, 118; Suarez, *De Remotione Parochorum,* p. 233.

ARTICLE IV. PENALTIES THAT MAY BE INFLICTED *Per Modum Praecepti*

Canon 1933, § 4, states that a penance, a penal remedy, an excommunication, a suspension and an interdict may be inflicted by way of precept without any judicial procedure, provided the offense is certain. This canon has lent itself to various interpretations. There are those who say that this enumeration is all-inclusive and therefore eliminates the infliction of any other canonical penalties under like circumstances by way of precept, except perhaps in the extraordinary event of cases for which a similar procedure seems indispensable,[50] while there are others who maintain that canon 1933, § 4, does not purport to present a complete list and therefore allows the infliction of other penalties as well, such as vindictive penalties and especially also all punishments which prove less severe than those of suspension or interdict.[51]

Roberti[52] holds that not only those penalties and remedies which are mentioned in canon 1933, § 4, may be inflicted by precept, but also any other penalty, as long as the Code does not specify that a special judicial procedure must be used. This interpretation permits the punishing of all delicts, even occult, so that occult crimes are punishable not only by a suspension *ex informata conscientia*[53] or by the administrative method of canon 2147, § 4, but also by way of precept. Such a method, he says, is sub-

---

[50] Coronata, *Institutiones,* III, n. 1453; *idem.,* "Pene e Procedimenti . . ."—Perfice Munus, VII (1932), 121-125; Noval, *De Processibus,* nn. 755, 756; *idem.,* "De Ratione Corrigendi ac Puniendi sive in Iudicio sive extra Iure Codicis J. C.,"—*Jus Pont.,* I-II (1921-1922), 147-156; III (1923), 36-40, 204-210.

[51] Chelodi, *Ius Poenale,* n. 25; Vermeersch-Creusen, *Epitome,* III, n. 258, 3o; Cappello, "Irrogatio Poenae per Modum Praecepti extra Iudicium,"—*Periodica,* XIX (1930), 36*-38*; Michiels, "De Reservatione Censurae Latae Sententiae Praecepto Peculiari Adnexae,"—*ETL,* IV (1927), 180-194, 613-619; Roberti, *De Delictis et Poenis,* nn. 257-262; *idem.,* "Quaenam Poenae Applicari Possint per Modum Praecepti,"—*Apollinaris,* IV (1931), 294-300.

[52] *Loc. cit.*

[53] Canons 2186-2193.

stantially that which was in vogue before the Code, and which at the present conforms to the practice of many ecclesiastical curias. The only penalties for the infliction of which he would demand a judicial trial are degradation, which implies a cleric's reduction to the lay state;[54] a cleric's perpetual deprivation of wearing the ecclesiastical garb;[55] a cleric's deposition, which implies his loss of ecclesiastical offices and his incapacity to attain to others;[56] a cleric's deprivation of holding a benefice to which he was appointed as an "irremovable" incumbent;[57] such penalties as are reserved to the competency of the Holy Office and its special norms of procedure for their imposition;[58] such penalties for the infliction of which a special administrative process is prescribed;[59] and, finally, the penal dismissal of religious.[60] All other penalties may be inflicted by way of precept.

Cappello[61] agrees with Roberti in the extension of the preceptive method of inflicting penalties beyond the limits of canon 1933, § 4. Relying on canon 2191, § 3, n. 3, he also permits this method of procedure when a judicial process is impossible, when such a trial would be absolutely useless, or when the good of souls demands it, because of the scandal or injury that would result from a criminal trial.

Another opinion, held by Chelodi[62] and Michiels,[63] states that the penalties mentioned in canon 1933, § 4, may be inflicted by precept; all other penalties besides those mentioned in that canon may be imposed by way of precept *ad instar legis* only.

Noval[64] limits the preceptive application of penalties to those cases which are expressly mentioned in canon 1933, § 4, and

---

[54] Canon 2305.
[55] Canon 2304.
[56] Canon 2303.
[57] Canon 1576, § 1.
[58] Canon 1557.
[59] Canons 2142-2194.
[60] Canons 649-668.
[61] "Irrogatio Poenae . . . ,"—*Periodica,* XIX (1930), 37*.
[62] *Loc. cit.*
[63] *Loc. cit.*
[64] "De Ratione Corrigendi . . . ,"—*Jus Pont.,* I-II (1921-1922), 155-156.

furthermore states that these penalties may be applied *per modum praecepti* only then when they are enacted as a result of a precept. This final limitation follows from the fact that he interprets the term *"inflicta sit ad modum praecepti particularis"* in the sense that these penalties are not only *inflicted* but also *constituted per modum praecepti.* This interpretation of Noval seems to be in harmony with the language and terminology used in the Code when speaking of penalties,[65] and is, as Roberti states, the strict interpretation, and the one best suited for measuring the scope and extent of the penal law of the Church.[66]

From the foregoing considerations it is evident that the problem has not been definitely solved. According to the wording of the law as it stands in canon 1933, § 4, it is apparent that there is question of the infliction of penalties, and in matters of opinion concerning penal affairs the less exacting among the tenable opinions has a prior right and claim to practical application.[67] The wording of canon 1933, § 4, does not demand an interpretation that connotes any greater comprehensiveness of canonical effects than that which has here been indicated in the view of Noval. The canon does not imply that the legislator wished to share any more extensive coercive powers with the ecclesiastical superior than those which have been predicated for him.[68] Had the legislator desired to be more generous than this in his grant of coercive powers to ecclesiastical superiors, it would have seemed equally as easy for him and perhaps much more spontaneous, simply to have stated that as long as the delict was certain there could be inflicted *per modum praecepti* any penalty whatever if for its infliction no special procedure was expressly required. Further, in canon 2291 it is stated: "Poenae vindicativae . . . *praesertim* sunt," and in canon 2310: *Praecipuae* poenitentiae

---

[65] Cf. Coronata, *Institutiones,* III, n. 1453, p. 378; IV, n. 1693, p. 84; Chelodi, *Ius Poenale,* n. 24, nota 1; Sole, *De Delictis et Poenis,* nn. 102, 103.

[66] "Quaenam Poenae Applicari . . . ,"—*Apollinaris,* IV (1931), 296; cf. also canon 19: "Leges quae poenam statuunt . . . strictae subsunt interpretationi."

[67] Canon 2219, § 1.

[68] Cf. Coronata, *Institutiones,* IV, n. 1453; Noval, "De Ratione Corrigendi . . . ,"—*Ius Pont.,* I-II (1921-1922), 155-156.

sunt"; such a non-restricting term is not, however, used in canon 1933, § 4. Were such a word used in this particular canon, the natural conclusion would be that the penalties mentioned in the canon are perhaps those which most commonly are inflicted, or those which are best suited for effecting the reform of the delinquent or the punishment of the crime, but in the absence of such a word, since the canon deals with penal matters, one is not justified in inserting that word in order to make the superior's coercive powers more extensive and inclusive. The arguments used by Roberti, namely, that the more extensive interpretation is preferable because it is in conformity with the practice of ecclesiastical curias and because it is substantially the practice in vogue before the Code, are not convincing. In regard to the former, he nowhere cites an instance of such an application. Finally, there is question here of the interpretation of a canon and not of the justification of something that may in reality be an abuse. As for the latter of his arguments, which points to a similar use of extensive coercive measures in the past, it is to be recalled that the Code declares as abrogated any and all of the past penal legislation of the Church if it is not given reexpression in the present Code.[69]

Cappello's contention that the provisions of canon 2191, § 3, n. 3, may be applied here, and thus grant the exercise of a more extensive penal power to the superior than is directly granted in canon 1933, § 4, is of rather doubtful force. The exceptions there made have been conceded in view of a special procedure, *suspensio ex informata conscientia,* and what is permitted in a particular instance cannot be applied in general.[70]

The penalty of excommunication which by canon 1933, § 4, the ecclesiastical superior is permitted to inflict, is always a censure; suspension and interdict, however, may be either a censure or a vindictive penalty.[71] Since canon 1933, § 4, uses the terms generically without qualification, it is to be concluded that suspen-

[69] Canon 6, n. 5; cf. Roberti, *De Delictis et Poenis,* n. 55.

[70] Canon 2219, § 3; Coronata, "Pene e Procedimenti . . ."—*Perfice Munus,* VII (1932), 121; Roberti, "Quaenam Poenae Applicari . . ."—*Apollinaris,* IV (1931), 299.

[71] Canon 2255, § 2.

sion and interdict may be inflicted either as a censure or as a vindictive penalty.[72]

In view of the foregoing considerations, the conclusion that only those penalties which are mentioned in canon 1933, § 4, may be inflicted and applied *per modum praecepti,* and then only when they are enacted as the result of a precept, seems fully recommended, since among the various opinions it reflects the closest conformity to, and the most intimate harmony with, the spirit which actuates all of the Church's penal legislation. Because of the various interpretations given to this question, one must agree with Roberti when the latter says that it is to be regretted that the Code has not been more explicit in determining the penalties that may be inflicted *per modum praecepti,* and that an authentic interpretation is to be desired.[73]

---

[72] Blat, *Commentarium,* IV, n. 477; Coronata, *Institutiones,* III, n. 1453; Cappello, "Irrogatio Poenae . . ."—*Periodica,* XIX (1930), 37*; Noval, "De Ratione Corrigendi . . ."—*Jus Pont.,* I-II (1921-1922), 155.

[73] "Quaenam Poenae Applicari . . ."—*Apollinaris,* IV (1931), 300.

CHAPTER X

EXTRAORDINARY PROCEDURE OF CANON 2222

ARTICLE I. IN CASE OF GRAVE SCANDAL OR SERIOUS TRANSGRESSION

Canon 2222, § 1, gives a practical norm of procedure in special cases, for it states that although there is no penalty attached to a law, the legitimate superior may, even without previous threat of penalty, punish its transgression with some just penalty, if the scandal given or the special gravity of the violation demands it. Under ordinary circumstances no penalty is to be inflicted for the violation of the divine or ecclesiastical law, if the Church's law does not decree a penalty. The derogation from the general rule of procedure consists in this, that a penalty may be inflicted upon a delinquent even though he was not previously notified and had no actual knowledge of its imminent infliction.[1] Ordinarily the delinquent is to be warned and threatened with a penalty, which is to be inflicted only in case of contumacy and failure to reform[2] Canon 2195 states that in the ecclesiastical sense, there is understood by a delict an external and morally imputable violation of the law to which at least an indeterminate canonical sanction is added. Since, however, the spiritual good of the Church demands a reparation of scandal and an atonement for the specially serious transgression of law, ecclesiastical superiors have been given the authority to act immediately in such cases.

The wording of the canon is very explicit as to its practical application; theoretically, however, there are various opinions. Although not really important to this work, it may be of interest to state briefly the opinions that exist. The controversy arises as the result of an effort to solve the seeming contradiction that exists between canon 2195, § 1, and canon 2222, § 1. One opinion[3]

---

[1] "Les Nouveautes du 'Codex,'" *L'Ami du Clerge,* XL (1923), 243.

[2] Canon 2222, § 1 . . .; secus . . ."

[3] Chelodi, *Ius Poenale,* nn. 2, 25; Salucci, *Diritto Penale,* I, 105; Sole, *De Delictis et Poenis,* nn. 6, 85.

looks upon canon 2195, § 1, as the norm or rule, and upon canon 2222, § 1, as an exception. A second opinion[4] concedes to the superior the right to add a sanction to a law already enacted, and thus the law is made retroactive even in its penal effect. Such an interpretation, however, pays scant heed to the age-old principle: *nullum crimen sine lege,* and abstracts from the necessary pre-existence of a penal law relative to the possible emergence of a canonical delict. A third opinion[5] not only holds that there can be no delict in the absence of a pre-existing penal law, but likewise contends that canon 2222, § 1, does not constitute any exception to the general rule of canon 2195, § 1. Roberti[6] points out that it is plainly possible for a legislator to realize that a certain act, although evil in itself, will disturb the social order in exceptionly cases only, which cases must be determined in a particular instance by the competent superior; hence, every ecclesiastical law, although it does not have attached thereto an explicit sanction, may be considered a penal law inasmuch as its transgression, whenever it is gravely scandalous, can be penalized according to law. The fact that the sanction of the law is indeterminate does not militate against its application, for, in conformity with the general law, it is left to the superior to determine the presence of serious scandal or of a specially grave transgression, and as a result, he is given the power to inflict an appropriate penalty according to the requirements of the individual case.

Whatever the correct theoretical explanation may be, it in no way interferes with the use of the power granted in the canon, for none of the proposed explanations denies to the legitimate superior the power that is granted to him in the canon law.

The reason for this special concession of power ultimately derives, as canon 2222, § 1, states, from the scandal and the special gravity of the transgression. In its theological sense scandal is

---

[4] Cicognani, *Canon Law,* 508, 557; Maroto, *Institutiones,* I, n. 184.

[5] Coronata, *Institutiones,* III, n. 1453; IV, n. 1638; Michiels, *Normae Generales,* I, 202-204; *idem.,* *De Delictis et Poenis,* 76-82; Roberti, *De Delictis et Poenis,* n. 53; Noval, "De Ratione Corrigendi . . ."—*Jus Pont.,* I-II (1921-1922), 147-156; III (1923), 36-40, 204-210; Vidal, "Notio Delicti in Iure Codicis,"—*Jus Pont.,* I-II (1921-1922), 99-102.

[6] *Loc. cit.*

any word or action which has the appearance at least of evil and is the occasion of sin for another. It may be caused either directly by being foreseen and intended, or indirectly by being foreseen but not intended.[7] The scandal here considered, however, must be notable and the gravity of the transgression exceptional, that is, the scandal must be more serious than that which ordinarily results from a grave and public transgression of law, and the gravity of the offense must be increased by the particular circumstances that surround an act.[8] A definite norm or rule to be used in determining exactly the presence of notable scandal or special malice cannot be given; there enter into the matter too many elements that can vary according to the place, the time, the rank of the delinquent, the character or subjective qualifications of the witnesses of the deed, and other similar factors. The superior must determine in his own mind whether or not the offense taken in itself and the circumstances surrounding it are sufficient to permit his use of the special power granted. This interpretation of the law is based on the fact that, if no exceptional scandal or gravity were here considered, this extraordinary power would not differ in any way from the power granted in canon 2221. This latter power grants to superiors who enjoy legislative competence, the right to enforce with a proper penalty—either by the enactment of a new penalty or by the intensification of an existing penalty—not merely their own laws and those of their predecessors, but also, in view of the specially attendant circumstances, the divine law and the ecclesiastical laws of a superior authority. Hence, the presence of such scandal as ordinarily is present upon the violation of a law would be sufficient to permit the establishment of a definite penalty or action by way of precept as outlined in the preceding chapter, but would not justify the use of the extraordinary powers of canon 2222, § 1.[9]

Although in accordance with this latter canon an ecclesiastical

---

[7] Marc-Gestermann-Raus, *Institutiones Morales Alphonsianae* (19. ed., 2 vols., Lugduni; Lutetiae Parisiorum, 1933), I, nn. 505-506.

[8] Ayrinhac-Lydon, *Penal Legislation,* p. 33; Coronata, *Institutiones,* IV, n. 1695; Pruemmer, *Manuale Iuris Canonici,* n. 564; Noval, "De Ratione Corrigendi . . . ,"—*Jus Pont.,* III (1923), 39.

[9] Noval, *loc. cit.*

superior may altogether dispense with the issuing of a threat of penalty before he actually inflicts the penalty, yet one may not in consequence of this ruling conclude that the canon disclaims all need of holding a judicial trial when the offense is public and when a trial can be conducted without any greater inconvenience than is normally entailed by the conduct of court proceedings.[10] The conditions surrounding the particular act that caused the scandal may, however, readily make the immediate infliction of punishment necessary. In the case of great scandal that notably disturbs the social order the public good demands that the delinquent be punished, rather than just corrected, as soon as possible. So also in the case of a very serious offense the good of the transgressor demands that some penalty be inflicted immediately, because thus alone will the special gravity of the crime be recognized and effectively punished. The assurance of such action on the part of the superior will naturally call for the most immediate method of precluding the danger of scandal and of averting the further disturbance of the social order.[11]

If, because of the exceptional gravity of a determinate case, a judicial trial is impractical or even impossible, then there is no obligation of following the strict procedure for the issuance of the precepts, for, since the legislator dispenses with the necessity of administering the admonition, he, as a result, dispenses also with the process which includes this admonition or threat of penalty. The superior may inflict the penalty, however, by means of a legal document or in the presence of two witnesses, in accordance with canon 24. This method of infliction is advisable, for, if the inflicted penalty needs to be later enforced by court action, then its imposition either by legal document or in the presence of two witnesses is a necessary precondition to render possible the opening of court proceedings.[12]

Finally, the punishment inflicted must be, in the words of canon 2222, § 1, a just one ("aliqua iusta poena"). Vermeersch-Creusen[13]

---

[10] Coronata, *Institutiones*, IV, n. 1695; Vermeersch-Creusen, *Epitome*, III, n. 412; Noval, "Re Ratione Corrigendi . . . ,"—*Jus Pont.*, I-II (1921-1922), 154; III (1923), 38.

[11] Noval, "De Ratione Corrigendi . . . ,"—*Jus Pont.*, III (1923), 39.

[12] Noval, "De Ratione Corrigendi . . . ,"—*Jus Pont.*, III (1923), 39.

[13] *Epitome*, III, n. 412.

and Noval[14] agree that since there is question of an extraordinary infliction of a penalty, this penalty should be less severe than those ordinarilly designated in law. The reason for this is that the delinquent had no way of previously knowing the penalty to which he was liable, inasmuch as its determination depended entirely on the will of the superior; also, because there was not given to him the opportunity to defend himself, as would be granted under ordinary conditions. As to its nature, there are those who say that the penalty could not be a censure, for a censure always demands contumacy which presupposes some previous warning, whether in the law itself or as specially enacted by the superior.[15] However, as pointed out in Chapter IX, Article III, neither canon 2233, § 2, nor canon 2242, § 3, demand this admonition under pain of invalidity. It may be easily possible for the superior to determine the lack of repentance or the presence of contumacy in ways other than the explicit threat of punishment. Since the terminology of canon 2222, § 1, is of a general nature, it can be said that not only a vindictive penalty but also a censure may be inflicted, according as the circumstances require.[16] If, however, the superior inflicts a vindictive penalty, he may not inflict such as are exclusively designated by the law itself for certain and definite offenses, as, for example, infamy of law (*infamia iuris*)[17] or an "irremovable" incumbent's deprivation of his benefice.[18]

ARTICLE II. PROBABLE OR "PRESCRIBED" DELICTS

Under ordinary conditions chastisement is not inflicted until the existence of a crime has been proved with moral certainty, nor after liability to punishment has lapsed through the interven-

---

[14] *Loc. cit.*

[15] Cappello, *De Censuris*, n. 26; Coronata, *Institutiones*, IV, n. 1695; Michiels, *Normae Generales*, I, 202; Vermeersch-Creusen, *Epitome*, III, n. 412.

[16] Rainer, *Suspension of Clerics*, 125.

[17] Canon 2293, § 2.

[18] Canon 2299, § 1. Cf. Michiels, *Normae Generales*, I, 202, nota 2.

tion of prescription.[19] When there is question of avoiding scandal, however, the law gives to the ecclesiastical superior a certain administrative, not penal, power, the exercise of which is not merely a right, but also a duty.[20]

The canon simply uses the term "legitimate Superior" (*"legitimus Superior"*). Undoubtedly the reason for this is the fact that there is question here of an extrajudicial procedure, and as such it is the legitimate ecclesiastical superior possessing coercive jurisdiction in the external forum in accordance with the prescription of canon 2220, to whom this extraordinary power is granted.[21]

The basis for action common to the three cases spoken of in this canon—withholding promotion to orders, prohibition to exercise the sacred ministry, removal from office—is either a probable crime[22] or a certain crime that is no longer subject to penal action because of legal prescription, while in the latter two cases the fear of, or the effort to avoid, scandal becomes a factor. A probable crime is one for which no full proof exists, but which has been testified to by at least one credible witness or is known to the superior from an extra-sacramental source.[23] Probability may be concerned with either the very fact of the offense's existence, or its imputability to a certain cleric.[24] Thus it may happen that a cleric is regarded as suspect, yet the proof that exists is not suffi-

---

[19] Canon 1704; Ayrinhac-Lydon, *Penal Legislation*, p. 61; "Les Nouveautes de 'Codex' "—*L'Ami du Clergé*, XL (1923), 243.

[20] Canon 2222, § 2: Pariter idem legitimus Superior, licet probabile tantum sit delictum fuisse commissum aut delicti certe commissi poenalis actio praescripta sit, non solum ius, sed etiam officium habet non promovendi clericum de cuius idoneitate non constat, et, ad scandalum evitandum, prohibendi clerico exercitium sacri ministerii aut etiam eundem ab officio, ad normam iuris, amovendi; quae omnia in casu non habent rationem poenae.

[21] Coronata, *Institutiones*, IV, n. 1696; *idem.*, "Pene e Procedimenti ad Modum Praecepti,"—*Perfice Munus*, VII (1932), 353.

[22] In this particular there is a similarity between canons 2222, § 2, and 2147, § 2, n. 4. In the latter canon it is decreed that an irremovable pastor is subject to removal for a probable occult crime that is imputed to him, if in view of this situation the ordinary judges with prudent foresight that it is possible for considerable resentment and offense to arise among the faithful.

[23] Augustine, *Commentary*, VIII, 87.

[24] Suarez, *De Remotione Parochorum*, p. 58.

cient to convict him in a criminal trial; if, in such an instance, according to the judgment of the superior there is the possibility that grave scandal will arise, he would be justified in acting to prevent it.[25] Equity, however, demands that a certain proportion be maintained between the probability of the offense attributed to a certain person and the gravity of the measures to be inflicted as a result of that probability; hence, not any sort of probability whatsoever is sufficient, but there is required the presence of positive and weighty arguments or reasons for suspecting a certain person or persons.[26] A crime is said to be certain if it can be proved by two trustworthy eyewitnesses who agree in the testimony presented;[27] it is probable if there exist serious reasons which point to a person's guilt.[28] In the determination of this probability the superior must use good judgment and prudence. He must not give too great credence, if any, to anonymous letters, nor must he neglect using means proper to the establishment of the charges made, lest calumny cause an innocent person to suffer. It will not, however, be advisable to reject entirely and immediately letters that are anonymous, or denunciations that are made privately, especially if the informant indicated means whereby the information proffered could be checked. It may be that recourse was had to such a procedure because of the desire to avoid undue complications or perhaps because of the lax preservation of secrets in similar past instances. If the accusation made is of great moment, then it would be proper for the superior, even when means for the checking of the information are not indicated, to institute a preliminary but very informal and secret investigation in order to safeguard the reputation of those concerned.[29]

The principle of prescription as applicable to delicts was definitely stated for the first time in 1898. Then time-limits were specified for certain determined crimes, while for certain other

---

[25] Coronata, "Pene e Procedimenti . . ."—*Perf. Munus,* VII (1932), 354.

[26] Coronata, "Pene e Procedimenti . . ."—*Perfice Munus,* VII (1932), 354; Suarez, *De Remotione Parochorum,* p. 58.

[27] Canon 1791, § 2.

[28] Connor, *The Administrative Removal of Pastors* (The Catholic University of America, Canon Law Studies, n. 104, Washington, D. C.: The Catholic University of America, 1937), p. 71.

[29] Suarez, *De Remotione Parochorum,* p. 58.

similarly determined crimes no duration of time however long was recognized as sufficient to justify the application of prescription.[30] The reasons for permitting prescription as applicable to certain crimes are readily understood. In the first place, the passage of an interval of time can easily extinguish the memory of the commission of the crime. To subject such a deed to criminal prosecution would merely disturb the public order anew and perhaps be the cause of much scandal. Secondly, lapse of time renders proof of, or defense against, an accusation rather difficult, with the result that there is, on the one hand, little likelihood of convicting a guilty person, and, on the other hand, great danger of condemning an innocent person.[31]

In the Code of Canon Law those crimes which are subject exclusively to the jurisdiction of the Holy Office for their prosecution are not prescriptible. These are schism, heresy and apostasy;[32] crimes which beget a suspicion of heresy;[33] superstition, magic, fortune-telling;[34] the making of false relics;[35] membership in societies which work against Church or State;[36] direct violation of the seal of confession,[37] and solicitation in confession.[38] Crimes other than these are limited as to the time during which judicial action can be brought. The ordinary period is three years.[39] Criminal action for injuries must be started within one year; such injuries would be outrages perpetrated against one's character, such as calumny and detraction, or the abuse of one's good name.[40] After five years criminal action can no longer be brought for qualified crimes[41] against the sixth commandment, such as sodomy

[30] S. C. Ep. et Reg., *Lublinen.*, 8 mart. 1898—*Fontes*, n. 2034.

[31] Chelodi, *Ius Poenale*, n. 120; Wernz-Vidal, *Ius Canonicum*, VI, 315.

[32] Canon 2312.

[33] Canons 2316; 2319, § 1, nn. 2, 3, 4; 2320; 2332; 2340, § 1; 2371.

[34] Canon 2325.

[35] Canon 2326.

[36] Canons 2335, 2336.

[37] Canon 2369, § 1.

[38] Canon 2368.

[39] Canon 1703.

[40] Noval, *De Processibus*, I, 275.

[41] The term "qualified crimes" against the sixth and seventh commandments is not explained in the Code, but it is interpreted by canonists to

or adultery,[42] and against the seventh commandment, such as sacrilegious theft.[43] For the crimes of simony and homicide a lapse of ten years is required before criminal action is prohibited because of prescription.[44]

In determining whether the time sufficient for prescription has elapsed, it is necessary also to examine the circumstances attending the case. If it is a crime consisting of a number of acts which serve as a means of carrying out an intention previously made (*delictum continuatum*), the acts are not taken separately, but they are considered as forming one crime, as, for example, in the making of false relics. In this case prescription begins with the placing of the last act only.[45] The crime may also be such as constitutes a "state" (*delictum permanens* or *successivum*). By the commission of the first act, which is a complete crime in itself, a condition is effected which perdures as long as the perpetrator remains in the state which the crime itself has induced, as, for example, the state of apostasy. Prescription in this type of crime begins with the day the crime ceases.[46] Finally, there is the habitual delict (*delictum collectivum* or *habituale*), which consists in an individual's repetition of the same acts which positive law considers as constituting only one crime, as, for example, the criminal practice of usury. In this instance the last act determines the point from which the time required for prescription is reckoned.[47]

Canon 2222, § 2, deals with a delict that was not punished judicially during a period of time allotted in law for such action,

---

mean crimes against the sixth and seventh commandments with which in the same act another crime is committed. Cf. Woywod, *Commentary,* II, n. 1665; Vermeersch-Creusen, *Epitome,* III, n. 138; Coronata, *Institutiones,* III, 1233.

[42] Canons 2357, 2359.

[43] Canon 2354.

[44] Canon 2392.

[45] Canon 1705, § 3. Coronata, *Institutiones,* IV, n. 1704; Roberti (*De Delictis et Poenis,* n. 198) considers the "*delictum continuatum*" under the category of the "*delictum permanens.*"

[46] Canon 1705, § 2; Coronata, *Institutiones,* IV, n. 1705; Roberti, *De Delictis et Poenis,* n. 198.

[47] Canon 1705, § 3; Coronata, *Institutiones,* IV, n. 1706; Roberti, *De Delictis et Poenis,* n. 199.

either because the superior neglected to act, or because the delinquent successfully avoided criminal prosecution, or for any other reason.[48] Due to circumstances now existing, the superior may find it necessary authoritatively to intervene, either for the sake of avoiding subsequent scandal to the faithful, or for the sake of preventing any loss of reputation to the guilty cleric.

The law of the Code imposes upon superiors the obligation of not promoting unworthy clerics to orders, an obligation that is emphatically stated. Canon 970 definitely and explicitly states that the ecclesiastical superior is given the power to prohibit, even extrajudicially, the promotion of any candidate to orders for any canonical cause whatever, while canon 973, § 3, demands moral certitude, derived from positive arguments and evidence, for the promotion of any cleric to orders. The reason for this can readily be seen. The honor of the sacred ministry must be the prime consideration. Were one who is of questionable character to be elevated to so great an office, it could easily happen that such action would react to the detriment of the sacred ministry, and instead of effecting the salvation of souls would rather produce scandal. If, therefore, the superior must refuse to promote a cleric whose worthiness is not evident, he must certainly be cautious when the worthiness of a cleric can be questioned because of a probable crime or in view of a certainly known crime which was committed remotely enough in the past to make its judicial prosecution impossible in the present due to legal prescription against this otherwise available remedy. Canon 2222, § 2, grants the lawful superior preventive power in such a case.[49] The superior must be careful to determine the degree of probability and to ascertain the defamation that is imminent, for it may be that through his refusal to promote a cleric to orders he brings upon that cleric a loss of good reputation hitherto enjoyed.[50] Refusal to promote to orders may at first appear to be a penal measure, but such it can-

---

[48] Roberti, *De Delictis et Poenis,* n. 277.

[49] Coronata, *Institutiones,* IV, n. 1696; *idem,* "Pene e Procedi-Corrigendi . . ."—*Jus Pont.,* III (1923), 209; Pistocchi, "De Superiore Potestatem Coactivam Habente"—*Il Monitore Ecclesiastico,* LXII (1937), 38, 39; Salucci, *Diritto Penale,* p. 110; Wernz-Vidal, *Ius Canonicum,* VII, n. 166.

[50] Vermeersch-Creusen, *Epitome,* III, n. 412.

not be, for no one has a strict right to be promoted to the clerical ranks although, once he has been so elevated, a positive reason seems necessary to withhold further promotion. The presence of a probable crime or of a certainly known but already "prescribed" crime is such a reason.[51]

If the ecclesiastical superior foresees that scandal is easily possible because of the existence of a probable crime attributed to a certain cleric, or because of a certainly known but already "prescribed" crime, he is justified, in an attempt to avoid scandal, in prohibiting the exercise of the sacred ministry to such a cleric. It matters not whether the crime referred to is of recent or remote origin; the gravity of the scandal resultant upon the knowledge of such a crime is the deciding factor. Since there is question here merely of a prohibition, it does not necessarily follow that acts placed contrary to this prohibition are invalid, although this invalidating effect may be attached to the prohibition; if it is, it must be expressly declared.[52] A superior may, therefore, simply prohibit the public exercise of the ministry if he feels that thereby the end for which the prohibition is imposed will be realized, namely, the avoidance of scandal; this method, if possible, would seem the more prudent and charitable, since the prohibition is not a penalty. Such a prohibition to exercise the ministry is spoken of by many authors as a *"suspensio ad cautelam."*[53]

For the imposition of this prohibition the Code prescribes no special form or procedure. Since there is no question of the infliction or the application of a penalty, a judicial procedure is not called for, although such a procedure may later become necessary due to additional evidence in the case of a probable crime. In order to be assured of the prohibition's execution and efficacy, however, proper administration would suggest that some precept or decree of suspension be issued, in which it is stated what

---

[51] Coronata, *Institutiones*, IV, n. 1696; *idem*, "Pene e Procedimenti . . ." —*Perfice Munus*, VII (1932), 353; Roberti, *De Delictis et Poenis*, n. 37.

[52] Coronata, *Institutiones*, IV, n. 1831; *idem*, "Pene e Procedimenti . . ." —*Perfice Munus*, VII (1932), 355.

[53] D'Annibale, *Summula Theol. Moral.*, I, n. 385; Lega, *De Delictis et Poenis*, n. 190; Pistocchi, "De Superiore Potestatem . . . ,"—*Il Monitore Eccl.*, LXII (1937), 39; Roberti, *De Delictis et Poenis*, n. 37.

exercise of the ministry is prohibited, whether that of orders, or that of jurisdiction, or the exercise of both, and further, that the measures therein imposed are not penal but merely administrative.[54] This precept may well be issued in the canonical form, namely, in the presence of two witnesses or as a legal document.[55] Removal from office, as permitted by this canon, is a matter of grave moment, and therefore should be prompted only in the face of equally grave reasons. The superior must prudently foresee the probability of great scandal to the faithful, a probability that naturally must be well founded. He should carefully weigh the nature and circumstances of the alleged crime, the number, character and motives of the informants, the personality and previous record of the cleric in question. If a pastor were prudently removed before full knowledge of a probable or of a certainly known but already "prescribed" crime came to the people, scandal would be averted to a great extent, the reputation of the pastor would more efficaciously be saved, and the good produced through his ministry would be given more permanent value.

The superior, however, may not proceed arbitrarily in any instance by ignoring the procedure ordinarily followed in these cases, but must act according to the specifications of law (*"ad normam iuris"*). The norms of law here referred to are undoubtedly those established in the law for the removal of a cleric from an office which he holds. Some offices are such *"simpliciter,"* as is the office of the notary, while others are attached to a benefice. For the removal of the former, no special procedure is specified, for these are removable *ad nutum.*[56] For the latter, however, the Code outlines a procedure for the removal of "irremovable" pastors,[57] of removable pastors[58] and of pastors who are removable *ad nutum,* as in the case of religious in the pastoral ministry.[59]

---

[54] Coronata, *Institutiones,* IV, 89, 260; *idem,* Pene e Procedimenti . . . ," —*Perfice Munus,* VII (1932), 355.

[55] Canons 24, 2225. Cf. Chap. IX, Art. III.

[56] Thus, for example, the Vicar General, Canon 366, § 2: "qui eum potest ad nutum removere."

[57] Canons 2147-2156; Connor, *Administrative Removal of Pastors,* 95-118.

[58] Canons 2157-2161; Connor, *Administrative Removal of Pastors,* 119-124.

[59] Canon 454, § 5.

These procedures must be followed, as is clearly stated in canon 2222, § 2.[60]

It must, however, be remembered that it is not for every crime, probable or already "prescribed," that a cleric may be removed according to the provisions of canon 2222, § 2. If it is a crime whose prosecution calls for its own definite and canonical process,[61] then this process is to be followed.[62] In the laws governing the procedure for an incumbent's removal from office in the case just delineated the legislator has made no distinction between public and occult, probable and certain, "prescribed" and "non-prescribed" crime. It is thus necessarily implied that the duly specified processes are always to be employed.

In all the above cases the means implemented by the superior are not of a penal but of an administrative nature. There is no question of the exacting of satisfaction or of the avenging of crime, for it may be that no crime has been committed at all, or, if it has been committed, that prescription bars any and all judicial cognizance of it. Nor can it be maintained that a correction of the delinquent is intended by the authoritative intervention. The professed aim is simply the avoidance of serious scandal, the promotion of the public honor and reverence due to the sacred ministry, or the salvation of souls in general.[63] As a consequence, if a cleric who is thus forbidden to exercise the sacred ministry were nevertheless to exercise his orders, he would not incur the irregularity that results from the exercise of an act of orders, when such an exercise was forbidden in view of a contracted canonical penalty.[64]

---

[60] Augustine, *Commentary,* VIII, 87; Cocchi, *Commentarium,* V, n. 32; Coronata, *Institutiones,* IV, n. 1696; Salucci, *Diritto Penale,* p. 111.

[61] Canons 2168-2185.

[62] Noval, *De Processibus,* II, n. 555.

[63] Chelodi, *Ius Poenale,* n. 25; Cocchi, *Commentarium,* V, n. 32; Noval, *De Processibus,* II, n. 554; Sole, *De Delictis et Poenis,* n. 91; Vermeersch-Creusen, *Epitome,* III, n. 412; Wernz-Vidal, *Ius Canonicum,* VII, n. 166.

[64] Canon 985, § 7; Augustine, *Commentary,* VIII, 87; Cocchi, *Commentarium,* V, n. 32.

CONCLUSIONS

The following items seek to set down in a summary fashion *some* of the conclusions which have been reached in the course of the study and composition of this dissertation:

1. While not using the terminology used at the present time, the early councils enacted laws that certainly expressed the principle of the *ipso facto* excommunication or penalty.

2. As a result of non-compliance with the legislation of the Council of Trent, all criminal cases involving bishops were without distinction eventually reserved to the exclusive competency of the Holy See.

3. Any penal power that was exercised by pastors as such in the past was based upon delegation or privilege, and was never generally considered as a power inherent in the pastoral office itself.

4. When correcting abuses existing in an exempt *"domus non formata,"* the bishop may use not only administrative decrees, but may also proceed to the infliction of penalties.

5. In view of the conflicting opinions of authors, and through the application of the norms of interpretation concerning penal matters, *latae sententiae* censures attached to particular precepts are to be considered reserved only then when the reservation is expressly stated.

6. An intermediate superior's attaching of a reserved censure to a delict which already connotes the attachment of a censure reserved to the Holy See is both illicit and invalid.

7. If a precept threatening a penalty has been imposed, the superior may proceed immediately, without further warning, to the infliction of the threatened penalty if the precept is violated.

8. The view that *per modum praecepti* there may be inflicted or applied only those penalties which are expressly mentioned in canon 1933, § 4, and then only when they were enacted by precept, appears as the one most conformable to the norms which govern the interpretation of the penal laws of the Code.

BIBLIOGRAPHY

Sources

Bullarii Romani Continuatio Summorum Pontificum, 19 vols., Prato, 1756-1883.

Bullarium Romanum, 25 vols., Augustae Taurinorum, 1857-1872.

Canones et Decreta Sacrosancti Oecumenici Concilii Tridentini, Romae: ex typographia polyglotta S. C. de Propaganda Fide, 1882.

Codicis Iuris Canonici Fontes cura Emi. Petri Card. Gasparri editi, 9 vols., Romae (Later, Civitate Vaticana): Typis Polyglottis Vaticanis, 1923-1939. (Vols. VII-IX ed. cura et studio Emi. Justiniani Card. Serédi.)

Collectanea Sacrae Congregationis de Propaganda Fide, 2 vols., Romae, 1907.

Collectio Lacensis, Acta et Decreta Conciliorum Recentiorum, 7 vols., Friburgi Brisgoviae, 1870-1890.

Corpus Iuris Canonici, ed. Lipsiensis 2., Aemilius Ludovicus Richter-Aemilius Friedberg, ed. anastatice repetita, 2 vols., Lipsiae: Tauchnitz, 1928.

Decretales D. Gregorii Papae IX, una cum Glossis Restitutae, Romae, 1582.

Denzinger, Henr. et Bannwart, Clem., *Enchiridion Symbolorum, Definitionum et Declarationum de Rebus Fidei et Morum,* 16. et 17. ed., Friburgi Brisgoviae: Herder, 1928.

Harduin, Jean, *Acta Conciliorum et Epistolae Decretales ac Constitutiones Summorum Pontificum,* 12 vols., Parisiis, 1714-1715.

Liber Sextus Decretalium, una cum Clementinis et Extravagantibus Earumque Glossis Restitutis, Romae, 1582.

Mansi, Joannes, *Sacrorum Conciliorum Nova et Amplissima Collectio,* 53 vols., Paris, Arnhem, Leipzig, 1901-1927.

Migne, P. J., *Patrologiae Cursus Completus—Series Latina,* 221 vols., Parisiis, 1844-1855.

Monumenta Germaniae Historica, Leges, 5 vols., I-IV ed. Pertz; V, ed. Pertz-Waitz-Brunner, Hanover, 1835-1889.

Reference Works

Ayrinhac, H. A., *Constitution of the Church in the New Code of Canon Law,* New York, 1925.

Ayrinhac, H. A., and Lydon, P. J., *Penal Legislation in the New Code of Canon Law,* revised edition, New York: Benziger, 1936.

[Bachofen], Charles Augustine, *A Commentary on the New Code of Canon Law,* 4. ed., 8 vols., St. Louis: B. Herder, 1921-1929.

———, *Compendium Iuris Regularium,* New York, 1903.

Barbosa, Augustinus, *Collectanea Doctorum tam Veterum quam Recentiorum in Jus Pontificium Universum,* 6 vols., in 3. Lugduni, 1716.

———, *De Officio et Potestate Episcopi,* 3 vols., Lugduni, 1656.

Benedictus XIV, *De Synodo Dioecesana,* 2 vols., Romae, 1806.

Blat, A., *Commentarium Textus Codicis Iuris Canonici,* 5 vols. in 6, Romae, 1921-1927.

Boehmer, J. H., *Jus Ecclesiasticum Protestantium,* 5. ed., 5 vols., Magdeburg, 1756.

Bouix, Dominicus, *Tractatus de Episcopo, ubi et de Synodo Dioecesana,* 2. ed., 2 vols., Parisiis, 1873.

———, *Tractatus de Papa, ubi et de Concilio Oecumenico,* 3 vols., Parisiis, 1869-1870.

———, *Tractatus de Iudiciis Ecclesiasticis,* 2 vols., Parisiis, 1855.

———, *Tractatus de Concilio Provinciali,* 2. ed., Parisiis, 1862.

Cappello, F., *Tractatus Canonico-Moralis de Censuris iuxta Codicem Iuris Canonici,* 3. ed., Taurinorum Augustae, Marietti, 1933.

———, *Summa Iuris Publici Ecclesiastici,* 2. ed., Romae: Apud Aedes Universitatis Gregorianae, 1928.

———, *Summa Iuris Canonici,* 3. ed., 3 vols., Romae, 1938.

Catholic Encyclopedia, The, 15 vols., and 2 supplements, New York: 1907-1922.

Cavagnis, Felix, *Institutiones Iuris Publici Ecclesiastici,* 2. ed., 2 vols., Romae, 1888.

Chelodi, J., *Ius de Personis,* 2. ed., Tridenti, 1921.

———, *Ius Poenale et Ordo Procedendi in Iudiciis Criminalibus juxta Codicem Iuris Canonici,* Tridenti, 1925.

Cicognani, Amleto, *Canon Law,* authorized English version, by J. O'Hara and F. Brennan, Philadelphia: Dolphin Press, 1934.

Claeys Bouuaert, F. et Simenon, G., *Manuale Iuris Canonici,* 3 vols., Gandae et Leodii, Vol. I and III, 4. ed., 1934; Vol. II, 2. ed., 1935.

Cocchi, Guidus, *Commentarium in Codicem Iuris Canonici ad Usum Scholarum,* 5 vols. in 8, Taurinorum Augustae, Vols. III-VII, 3. ed., Vol. II et VIII, 4. ed., Vol. I, 5. ed., Augustae Taurinorum: Marietti, 1931-1938.

Connor, Maurice, *The Administrative Removal of Pastors,* The Catholic University of America, Canon Law Studies, n. 104, Washington, D. C.: The Catholic University of America, 1937.

Coronata, Matthaeus Conte a, *Institutiones Iuris Canonici,* 5 vols., Taurini: Marietti, Vols. I et II, 1939; Vol. III, 1933; Vol. IV, 1935; Vol. V, 1936.

D'Annibale, J., *Summula Theologiae Moralis,* 5. ed., 3 vols., Romae, 1908.

De Meester, Alphonsus, *Juris Canonici et Juris Canonico-Civilis Compendium,* nova ed., 3 vols. in 4, Brugis, 1921-1928.

Droste, F.,-Messmer, S., *Canonical Procedure in Disciplinary and Criminal Cases of Clerics,* New York, 1887.

Eichman, Eduard, *Das Strafrecht des Codex Iuris Canonici,* Paderborn, 1920.

———, *Lehrbuch des Kirchenrechts auf Grund des Codex Iuris Canonici,* 2. ed., Paderborn: Schoeningh, 1926.

Fagnanus, Prosper, *Commentarium in Quinque Libros Decretalium,* 4 vols., Venetiis, 1696.

Ferraris, F. Lucius, *Prompta Bibliotheca, Canonica, Iuridica, Moralis, Theologica, necnon Ascetica, Polemica, Rubricistica, Historica,* 9 vols., Romae, 1885-1899; Vol. IX, ed. Bucceroni.

Ferreres, Joannes, *Institutiones Canonicae,* 2. ed., 2 vols., Barcinone, 1920.

Fournier, Edouard, *Les Origines du Vicaire General,* Paris, 1922.

Fournier, Paul, *Les Officialites au Moyen Age, Paris,* 1880.

Genicot, E., et Salsmans, I., *Institutiones Theologiae Moralis,* 11. ed., 2 vols., Bruxellis, 1927.

Gonzalez-Tellez, Emmanuel, *Commentaria Perpetua in Singulos Textus Quinque Librorum Decretalium Gregorii IX,* 5 vols. in 4, Lugduni, 1715.

Hefele, Carl, *Konciliengeschichte,* 9 vols. (vols. VIII and IX continued by Card. Hergenroether), Freiburg im Breisgau, 1873-1890.

Hinschius, Paul, *Das Kirchenrecht der Katholiken und Protestanten in Deutschland,* 6 vols., Berlin, 1869-1897. Vols. I-IV, *System des katholischen Kirchenrechts,* Berlin, 1869-1888.

Hollweck, Joseph, *Die kirchlichen Strafgesetze,* Mainz, 1899.

Hostiensis, Cardinalis (Henricus de Segusio), *Commentaria in Quinque Decretalium Libros,* 5 vols. in 3, Venetiis, 1581.

———, *Summa Aurea,* Venetiis, 1570.

Kienitz, Erwin von, *Generalvikar und Offizial auf Grund des Codex Iuris Canonici,* Freiburg im Breisgau: Herder, 1931.

Kober, F., *Dis Suspension der Kirchendiener,* Tuebingen, 1862.

———, *Der Kirchenbann nach den Grundsaetzen des canonischen Rechts,* Tuebingen, 1863.

———, *Deposition und Degradation nach den Grundsaetzen des kirchlichen Rechts,* Tuebingen, 1867.

Lega, Michael, *Praelectiones in Textum Iuris Canonici—De Delictis et Poenis,* 2. ed., Romae, 1910.

———, *De Iudiciis Ecclesiasticis,* 4 vols., Romae, 1896-1901.

Leo XIII, Great Encyclical Letters of, New York: Benziger, 1903.

Marc, C.-Gestermann, F.-Raus, J., *Institutiones Morales Alphonsianae,* 19. ed., 2 vols., Lugduni, Lutetiae Parisiorum, 1933.

Maroto, P., *Institutiones Iuris Canonici ad Normam Novi Codicis,* 2 vols., Madrid, 1919.

Michiels, G., *Normae Generales Iuris Canonici,* 2 vols., Lublin-Polonia, 1929.

———, *De Delictis et Poenis,* Lublin-Polonia, 1934.

Moriarity, F., *The Extraordinary Absolution from Censures,* The Catholic University of America, Canon Law Studies, n. 113, Washington D. C.: The Catholic University of America, 1938.

Noldin, H.-Schmitt, A., *Summa Theologiae Moralis*, 26. ed., 3 vols., Oeniponte, 1939.

Noval, Joseph, *Commentarium Codicis Iuris Canonici, Lib. IV, De Processibus*, 2 vols., Romae, 1920-1932.

Ottaviani, Alaphridus, *Institutiones Iuris Publici Ecclesiastici*, 2. ed., 2 vols., Typis Polyglottis Vaticanis, 1936.

Panormitanus, Abbas (Nicolaus de Tudeschis), *Commentaria in Quinque Libros Decretalium*, 5 vols. in 7, Venetiis, 1588

Phillips, George, *Kirchenrecht*, 7 vols., Regensburg, 1845-1872.

Piatus Montensis, *Praelectiones Iuris Regularis*, 3. ed., 2 vols., Tornaci (?).

Pruemmer, Dominicus, *Manuale Iuris Canonici*, 4. et 5. eds., Friburgi Brisgoviae, 1927.

Rainer, Eligius, *Suspension of Clerics*, The Catholic University of America, Canon Law Studies, n. 111, Washington, D. C.: The Catholic University of America, 1937.

Reiffenstuel, A., *Ius Canonicum Universum*, 5 vols. in 7, Parisiis, 1864-1870.

Roberti, Franciscus, *De Delictis et Poenis*, Romae, 1938.

Salucci, Raffaele, *Il Diritto Penale Secondo il Codice di Diritto Canonico*, 2 vols., Subiaco, 1926-1930.

Schaefer, T., O.M. Cap., *De Religiosis ad Normam Codicis Iuris Canonici*, Muenster, 1927.

Schmalzgrueber, Franc., *Ius Ecclesiasticum Universum*, 5 vols. in 12, Romae, 1843-1845.

Schroeder, Alfred, *Entwicklung des Archidiakonats*, Augsburg, 1890.

Sole, Jacobus, *De Delictis et Poenis*, Romae, 1920.

Suarez, Emmanuale, *De Remotione Parochorum Aliisque Processibus Tertiae Partis Lib. IV Cod. Iur. Can.*, Romae, 1931.

Suarez, Franciscus, *Opera Omnia*, ed. Ludovicus Vives, 26 vols., Parisiis, 1861; Vol. XXIII, *De Censuris in Communi.*

Thomas Aquinas, St., *Commentaria in Quatuor Libros Sententiarum Petri Lombardi*, Paris, 1659.

Thomassinus, Ludovicus, *Vetus et Nova Ecclesiae Disciplinae circa Beneficia et Beneficiarios*, Moguntiaci, 1787.

Tobin, Thomas, *De Officiali Curiae Dioecesanae*, Romae: Apud Aedes Pontificiae Universitatis Gregorianae, 1936.

Toso, Albertus, *Ad Codicem Iuris Canonici Commentaria Minora*, 5 vols., Romae: Marietti, 1920-1934.

Van Hove, A., *Commentarium Lovaniense in Codicem Iuris Canonici*, Vol. II, *De Legibus Ecclesiasticis*, Mechliniae: H. Dessain, 1930.

Vermeersch, A.-Creusen, J., *Epitome Iuris Canonici*, 3 vols., Mechliniae: H. Dessain, Vol. I, 6. ed., 1937; Vol. II, 5. ed., 1934; Vol. III, 5. ed., 1936.

Wernz, Franc., *Ius Decretalium*, 2. ed., 6 vols., Romae, 1906-1913.

Wernz, F.-Vidal, P., *Ius Canonicum*, 7 tom. in 8 vols., Romae: Apud Aedes Universitatis Gregorianae, 1923-1938.

Woywod, Stan., *A Practical Commentary on the Code of Canon Law*, 4. ed., 2 vols., New York: Wagner, 1932.

ARTICLES

. . . "Les Nouveautes de 'Codex,'"—*L'Ami du Clergé*, XL (1923), 243-244.

Cappello, F., "De absolutione a censuris 'Ab Homine' ac de metu relate ad censuras,"—*NRT*, XLVII (1920), 525-531.

———, "Irrogatio Poenae per Modum Praecepti extra Iudicium,"—*Periodica*, XIX (1930), 36*-38*.

Coronata, Matthaeus Conte a, "Pene e Procedimenti ad Modum Praecepti," —*Perfice Munus*, VII (1932), 34-38, 121-125, 192-200, 270-273, 352-356.

Creusen, J., "De Reservatione Censurae Praecepto Latae,"—*Jus Pont.*, IV (1924), 26-29.

———, "La reserve des censures 'ab homine,'"—*NRT*, LV (1928), 436-444.

Kraemer, P., "An ius visitandi domos vel saltem Ecclesias Regularium Ordinariis loci competat,"—*CpR*, IX (1928), 245-248.

Meysztowicz, V., "Domicilium et Quasi-Domicilium Eorumque Effectus in Codice Juris Canonici,"—*Jus Pont.*, VI (1926), 34-55, 112-126, 154-158.

Michiels, G., "De reservatione censurae latae sententiae praecepto peculiari adnexae,"—*ETL*, IV (1927), 180-194, 613-619.

Noval, J., "De ratione corrigendi ac puniendi sive in iudicio sive extra iure Codicis J. C.,"—*Jus Pont.*, I-II (1921-1922), 147-156; III (1923), 36-40, 204-210.

Pistocchi, M., "De Superiore potestatem coactivam Habente,"—*Il Monitore Ecclesiastico*, IX (1937), 35-41, 141-151, 235-244.

Roberti, F., "Quaenam Poenae applicari possint per modum Praecepti,"—*Apollinaris*, IV (1931), 294-300.

———, "An censura latae sententiae per praeceptum constituta sit reservata," —*Apollinaris*, VI (1933), 341-348.

Teodori, I., "Peregrini quoad censuras,"—*Apollinaris*, IV (1931), 139-141.

Van Hove, A., "Leges quae ordini publico consulunt,"—*ETL*, I (1924), 156-159.

PERIODICALS

Apollinaris, Romae, 1928—

Commentarium pro Religiosis (later *Commentarium pro Religiosis et Missionariis*), Romae, 1920—

Ephemerides Theologicae Lovanienses, Lovanii, 1924—

Jus Pontificium, Romae, 1921—

L'Ami du Clergé, Paris, 1878—

Monitore Ecclesiastico, Il, Romae, 1876—

Nouvelle Revue Théologique, Paris, 1869—

Perfice Munus, Torino, 1926—

Periodica de Re Canonica et Morali utili Praesertim Religiosis et Missionariis, Brugis, 1905—

Abbreviations

AAS—*Acta Apostolicae Sedis.*
ASS—*Acta Sanctae Sedis.*
Coll. Lac.—*Collectio Lacensis, Acta et Decreta Conciliorum Recentiorum.*
CpR—*Commentarium pro Religiosis et Missionariis.*
ETL—*Ephemerides Theologicae Lovanienses.*
Fontes—*Codicis Iuris Canonici Fontes cura . . . Gasparri editi.*
Harduin—*Acta Conciliorum* etc.
Jus Pont.—*Jus Pontificium.*
Mansi—*Sacrorum Conciliorum Nova et Amplissima Collectio.*
MPG—Migne, *Patrologia Graeca.*
MPL—Migne, *Patrologia Latina.*
NRT—*Nouvelle Revue Théologique.*
Periodica—*Periodica de Re Canonica et Morali Utili praesertim Religiosis et Missionariis.*

BIOGRAPHICAL NOTE

ANTHONY ALBERT ESSWEIN was born on September 29, 1910, at Saint Louis, Missouri. After receiving his primary education in Saint Anthony School there, he attended the Christian Brothers High School of the same city. Upon his graduation from the latter institution he entered the Kenrick Theological Seminary at Webster Groves, Missouri. He was ordained to the Sacred Priesthood on June 6, 1937. In 1938 he entered the Canon Law School of the Catholic University of America at Washington, D. C., where he obtained the Baccalaureate in June, 1939, and the Licentiate in June, 1940.

ALPHABETICAL INDEX

Abbots *nullius,* coercive power, 24, 63.
Absence
  from territory and subjection to coercive power, 68.
  from convent, 87.
Administrator, coercive power, 68.
Admonitions,
  in history, 27, 34.
  as penal remedy, 102.
  after giving of a precept, 108.
Alexander III, Pope, 48.
Apostates, subjection to local ordinary, 87.
Apostolic Administrator, coercive power, 64.
Archbishop, see Metropolitan.
Archdeacon,
  coercive powers of, 37.
  appointment of assistants, 41.
  infliction of excommunication, 40.
  iudex ordinarius, 39.
  Tridentine legislation, 41.

Bishop,
  coercive powers, 25, 65.
  consultation with priests, 25, 26, 29.
  criminal case against, 10.
  possesses ordinary power, 66.
Boniface VIII, 5.

Cardinals,
  coercive power, 57.
  suburbicarian, 58.
Causa Maiores,
  essential, 54.
  per accidens, 55.
  per se, 55.
  reserved to Pontiff, 10, 14, 54.
Censure,
  conditionally inflicted, 78.
  latae sententiae, 28.
  latae sententiae ab homine, 96.
  reservation of, 94.
Chrodegang, St., Regulations of, 38.
Church,
  a perfect society, 1.
  coercive powers, 3.
Congregations, Sacred,
  coercive power, 58.
  general decrees, 58.
  particular decrees, 59.
Consultors, Diocesan,
  coercive powers, 68.
  power held collegiately, 69.

Delicts, probable or prescribed, 119.
Diocesan Right, Congregations of, 83.
Divine Office, method of recitation in province, 19, 22.
Document, legal, 107.
Domicile,
  basis of subjection to coercive power, 73.
  acquisition of, 73.
  change of and subjection to coercive power, 78.

Ecumenical Council, coercive power, 56.
Exclaustration and subjection to coercive power of local ordinary, 74.
Excommunication,
  bishop's subjection to, 14.
  inflicted by way of precept, 110.

Febronius, 8.
Fugitive and subjection to local ordinary, 87.

Gregory the Great and episcopal coercive power, 29.

Hincmar of Rheims, 20.

Incardination and subjection to coercive power, 29.
Interdict, inflicted by way of precept, 110.

Jurisdiction,
  definition, 50.
  division, 50.
  coercive power of superior when outside territory, 101.
  requisite for inflicting penalties, 50.

Lateran, IV General Council of, and episcopal coercive power, 32.

Marsilius of Padua, 5.
Mendicants and coercive power of local ordinary, 92.

Metropolitan,
appeals to, 19.
coercive power of, 11, 60.
power over suffragans, 13, 19, 21, 22.
visitation of diocese of suffragan, 23, 60.

Office, removal from, 126.
Officialis,
coercive powers, history, 44.
coercive powers under Code, 71.
required special mandate, 45.
special coercive powers,
slander, 45.
summoning of witnesses, 46, 72.
Orders, exercise of barred to unworthy, 35, 124.
Orders, reception of, forbidden to unworthy candidates, 35, 124.

Passionists and privilege of exemption, 84.
Pastor,
coercive power, 48, 51.
not a *iudex ordinarius,* 49.
Patriarch,
authority over Metropolitans, 17, 60.
coercive power, 16, 60.
court of appeal, 17.
rights determined by Benedict XIV, 17.
Patriarchates, five, 16.
Penal remedies inflicted by way of precept, 110.
Penalties,
inflicted *per modum praecepti,* 110.
reservation of, 94.
Peregrini, subjection to coercive power, local ordinary, 79.
Personal laws, 77.
Pistoia, Council of, 6.
Plenary Council,
coercive power, 61.
approval in "forma communis," 63.
Pontifical Right, Congregations of, 84.
Pope,
coercive power,
pre-Code, 8.
Code law, 53.
Precept, penalties by way of, 106, 125.
Prefects Apostolic, 24, 63.
Prescription and crimes, 120.
Probable delict, 120.
Provincial council,
coercive power, 61.
approval in "forma communis," 63.
Provincial synod,
trial of bishop, 10.
consulted by metropolitan, 23.
Pseudo-Isidorian Decretals, 10.
Public Order, laws concerning, 80.

Quasi-domicile,
basis of subjection to coercive power, 73.
acquisition of, 74.

Redemptorists and privilege of exemption, 84.
Religious, Exempt,
subject to local ordinary, 32, 64, 83.
crimes in *domus formata,* 85.
crimes in *domus non formata,* 85.
legitimate absence from convent, 86.
illegitimate absence from convent, 87.
Reservation of penalties, 94.
when already reserved to Holy See, 99.
Residence, violation of law of, 77.

Scandal,
and public order, 80.
grave, reason for extraordinary procedure, 115.
Secularization and subjection to coercive power of local ordinary, 75.
Sins, capital, 25, 27.
Suspension,
subjection of bishop to, 14.
inflicted by way of precept, 110.
Suspension *"ad cautelam,"* 35, 125.
Synod, Bishop is sole legislator, 67.

Transients, subjection to penal laws, 79.

Vagi, subjection to coercive power, 73.
Vicar Apostolic, coercive power, 24, 63.
Vicar Capitular, coercive power, 68.
Vicar General,
coercive power, in history, 42.
coercive power, under Code, 70.
special mandate required, 43.
Visitation of diocese of suffragan by Metropolitan, 23.

CANON LAW STUDIES

1. Freriks, Rev. Celestina A., C.PP.S., J.C.D., Religious Congregations in Their External Relations, 121 pp., 1916.
2. Galliher, Rev. Daniel M., O.P., J.C.D., Canonical Elections, 117 pp., 1917.
3. Borkowski, Rev. Aurelius L., O.F.M., J.C.D., De Confraternitatibus Ecclesiasticis, 136 pp., 1918.
4. Castillo, Rev. Cayo, J.C.D., Disertacion Historico-Canonica sobre la Potestad del Cabildo en Sede Vacante o Impedida del Vicario Capitular, 99 pp., 1919 (1918).
5. Kubelbeck, Rev. William J., S.T.B., J.C.D., The Sacred Penitentiaria and Its Relation to Faculties of Ordinaries and Priests, 129 pp., 1918.
6. Petrovits, Rev. Joseph, J.C., S.T.D., J.C.D., The New Church Law on Matrimony, X-461 pp., 1919.
7. Hickey, Rev. John J., S.T.B., J.C.D., Irregularities and Simple Impediments in the New Code of Canon Law, 100 pp., 1920.
8. Klekotka, Rev. Peter J., S.T.B., J.C.D., Diocesan Consultors, 179 pp., 1920.
9. Wanenmacher, Rev. Francis, J.C.D., The Evidence in Ecclesiastical Procedure Affecting the Marriage Bond, 1920 (Printed 1935).
10. Golden, Rev. Henry Francis, J.C.D., Parochial Benefices in the New Code, IV-119 pp., 1921 (Printed 1925).
11. Koudelka, Rev. Charles J., J.C.D., Pastors, Their Rights and Duties According to the New Code of Canon Law, 211 pp., 1921.
12. Melo, Rev. Antonius, O.F.M., J.C.D., De Exemptione Regularium, X-188 pp., 1921.
13. Schaaf, Rev. Valentine Theodore, O.F.M., S.T.B., J.C.D., The Cloister, X-180 pp., 1921.
14. Burke, Rev. Thomas Joseph, S.T.D., J.C.D., Competence in Ecclesiastical Tribunals, IV-117 pp., 1922.
15. Leech, Rev. George Leo, J.C.D., A Comparative Study of the Constitution "Apostolicae Sedis" and the "Codex Juris Canonici," 179 pp., 1922.
16. Motry, Rev. Hubert Louis, S.T.D., J.C.D., Diocesan Faculties According to the Code of Canon Law, II-167 pp., 1922.
17. Murphy, Rev. George Lawrence, J.C.D., Delinquencies and Penalties in the Administration and the Reception of the Sacraments, IV-121 pp., 1923.
18. O'Reilly, Rev. John Anthony, S.T.B., J.C.D., Ecclesiastical Sepulture in the New Code of Canon Law, II-129 pp., 1923.
19. Michalicka, Rev. Wenceslas Cyrill, O.S.B., J.C.D., Judicial Procedure in Dismissal of Clerical Exempt Religious, 107 pp., 1923.

20. Dargin, Rev. Edward Vincent, S.T.B., J.C.D., Reserved Cases According to the Code of Canon Law, IV-103 pp., 1924.
21. Godfrey, Rev. John A., S.T.B., J.C.D., The Right of Patronage According to the Code of Canon Law, 153 pp., 1924.
22. Hagedorn, Rev. Francis Edward, J.C.D., General Legislation on Indulgences, II-154 pp., 1924.
23. King, Rev. James Ignatius, J.C.D., The Administration of the Sacraments to Dying Non-Catholics, V-141 pp., 1924.
24. Winslow, Rev. Francis Joseph, M.M., J.C.D., Vicars and Prefects Apostolic, IV-149 pp., 1924.
25. Correa, Rev. Jose Servelion, S.T.L., J.C.D., La Potestad Legislativa de la Iglesia Catolica, IV-127 pp., 1925.
26. Dugan, Rev. Henry Francis, A.M., J.C.D., The Judiciary Department of the Diocesan Curia, 87 pp., 1925.
27. Keller, Rev. Charles Frederick, S.T.B., J.C.D., Mass Stipends, 167 pp., 1925.
28. Paschang, Rev. John Linus, J.C.D., The Sacramentals According to the Code of Canon Law, 129 pp., 1925.
29. Pointek, Rev. Cyrillus, O.F.M., S.T.B., J.C.D., De Indulto Exclaustrationis necnon Saecularizationis, XIII-289 pp., 1925.
30. Kearney, Rev. Richard Joseph, S.T.B., J.C.D., Sponsors at Baptism According to the Code of Canon Law, IV-127 pp., 1925.
31. Bartlett, Rev. Chester Joseph, A.M., LL.B., J.C.D., The Tenure of Parochial Property in the United States of America, V-108 pp., 1926.
32. Kilker, Rev. Adrian Jerome, J.C.D., Extreme Unction, V-425 pp., 1926.
33. McCormick, Rev. Robert Emmett, J.C.D., Confessors of Religious, VIII-266 pp., 1926.
34. Miller, Rev. Newton Thomas, J.C.D., Founded Masses According to the Code of Canon Law, VII-93 pp., 1926.
35. Roelker, Rev. Edward G., S.T.D., J.C.D., Principles of Privilege According to the Code of Canon Law, XI-166 pp., 1926.
36. Bakalarczyk, Rev. Richardus, M.I.C., J.U.D., De Novitiatu, VIII-208 pp., 1927.
37. Pizzuti, Rev. Lawrence, O.F.M., J.U.L., De Parochis Religiosis, 1927. (Not Printed.)
38. Bliley, Rev. Nicholas Martin, O.S.B., J.C.D., Altars According to the Code of Canon Law, XIX-132 pp., 1927.
39. Brown, Mr. Brendan Francis, A.B., LL.M., J.U.D., The Canonical Juristic Personality with Special Reference to its Status in the United States of America, V-212 pp., 1927.
40. Cavanaugh, Rev. William Thomas, C.P., J.U.D., The Reservation of the Blessed Sacrament, VIII-101 pp., 1927.
41. Doheny, Rev. William J., C.S.C., A.B., J.U.D., Church Property: Modes of Acquisition, X-118 pp., 1927.
42. Feldhaus, Rev. Aloysius H., C.PP.S., J.C.D., Oratories, IX-141 pp., 1927.

43. Kelly, Rev. James Patrick, A.B., J.C.D., The Jurisdiction of the Simple Confessor, X-208 pp., 1927.
44. Neuberger, Rev. Nicholas J., J.C.D., Canon 6 or the Relation of the Codex Juris Canonici to the Preceding Legislation, V-95 pp., 1927.
45. O'Keefe, Rev. Gerald Michael, J.C.D., Matrimonial Dispensations, Powers of Bishops, Priests, and Confessors, VIII-232 pp., 1927.
46. Quigley, Rev. Joseph A. M., A.B., J.C.D., Condemned Societies, 139 pp., 1927.
47. Zaplotnik, Rev. Johannes Leo, J.C.D., De Vicariis Foraneis, X-142 pp., 1927.
48. Duskie, Rev. John Aloysius, A.B., J.C.D., The Canonical Status of the Orientals in the United States, VIII-196 pp., 1928.
49. Hyland, Rev. Francis Edward, J.C.D., Excommunication, Its Nature, Historical Development and Effects, VIII-181 pp., 1928.
50. Reinmann, Rev. Gerald Joseph, O.M.C., J.C.D., The Third Order Secular of Saint Francis, 201 pp., 1928.
51. Schenk, Rev. Francis J., J.C.D., The Matrimonial Impediments of Mixed Religion and Disparity of Cult, XVI-318 pp., 1929.
52. Coady, Rev. John Joseph, S.T.D., J.U.D., A.M., The appointment of Pastors, VIII-150 pp., 1929.
53. Kay, Rev. Thomas Henry, J.C.D., Competence in Matrimonial Procedure, VIII-164 pp., 1929.
54. Turner, Rev. Sidney Joseph, C.P., J.U.D., The Vow of Poverty, XLIX-217 pp., 1929.
55. Kearney, Rev. Raymond A., A.B., S.T.D., J.C.D., The Principles of Delegation, VII-149 pp., 1929.
56. Conran, Rev. Edward James, A.B., J.C.D., The Interdict, V-163 pp., 1930.
57. O'Neill, Rev. William H., J.C.D., Papal Rescripts of Favor, VII-218 pp., 1930.
58. Bastnagel, Rev. Clement Vincent, J.U.D., The Appointment of Parochial Adjutants and Assistants, XV-257 pp., 1940.
59. Ferry, Rev. William A., A.B., J.C.D., Stole Fees, V-136 pp., 1930.
60. Costello, Rev. John Michael, A.B., J.C.D., Domicile and Quasi-Domicile, VII-201 pp., 1930.
61. Kremer, Rev. Michael Nicholas, A.B., S.T.B., J.C.D., Church Support in the United States, VI-136 pp., 1930.
62. Angulo, Rev. Luis, C.M., J.C.D., Legislation de la Iglesia sobre la intencion en la application de la Santa Misa, VII-104 pp., 1931.
63. Frey, Rev. Wolfgang Norbert, O.S.B., A.B., J.C.D., The Act of Religious Profession, VIII-174 pp., 1931.
64. Roberts, Rev. James Brendan, A.B., J.C.D., The Banns of Marriage, XIV-140 pp., 1931.
65. Ryder, Rev. Raymond Aloysius, A.B., J.C.D., Simony, IX-151 pp., 1931.
66. Campagna, Rev. Angelo, Ph.D., J.U.D., Il Vicario Generale del Vescovo, VII-205 pp., 1931.

67. Cox, Rev. Joseph Godfrey, A.B., J.C.D., The Administration of Seminaries, VI-124 pp., 1931.
68. Gregory, Rev. Donald J., J.U.D., The Pauline Privilege, XV-165 pp., 1931.
69. Donohue, Rev. John F., J.C.D., The Impediment of Crime, VII-110 pp., 1931.
70. Dooley, Rev. Eugene A., O.M.I., J.C.D., Church Law on Sacred Relics, IX-143 pp., 1931.
71. Orth, Rev. Clement Raymond, O.M.C., J.C.D., The Approbation of Religious Institutes, 171 pp., 1931.
72. Pernicone, Rev. Joseph M., A.B., J.C.D., The Ecclesiastical Prohibition of Books, XII-267 pp., 1932.
73. Clinton, Rev. Connell, A.B., J.C.D., The Paschal Precept, IX-108 pp., 1932.
74. Donnelly, Rev. Francis B., A.M., S.T.L., J.C.D., The Diocesan Synod, VIII-125 pp., 1932.
75. Torrente, Rev. Camilo, C.M.F., J.C.D., Las Processiones Sagradas, V-145 pp., 1932.
76. Murphy, Rev. Edwin J., C.PP.S., J.C.D., Suspension Ex Informata Conscientia, XI-122 pp., 1932.
77. MacKenzie, Rev. Eric F., A.M., S.T.L., J.C.D., The Delict of Heresy in Its Commission, Penalization, Absolution, VII-124 pp., 1932.
78. Lyons, Rev. Avitus E., S.T.B., J.C.D., The Collegiate Tribunal of First Instance, XI-147 pp., 1932.
79. Connolly, Rev. Thomas A., J.C.D., Appeals, XI-195 pp., 1932.
80. Sangmeister, Rev. Joseph V., A.B., J.C.D., Force and Fear as Precluding Matrimonial Consent, V-211 pp., 1932.
81. Jaeger, Rev. Leo A., A.B., J.C.D., The Administration of Vacant and Quasi-Vacant Episcopal Sees in the United States, IX-229 pp., 1932.
82. Rimlinger, Rev. Herbert T., J.C.D., Error Invalidating Matrimonial Consent, VII-79 pp., 1932.
83. Barrett, Rev. John D. M., S.S., J.C.D., A Comparative Study of the Third Plenary Council of Baltimore and the Code, IX-221 pp., 1932.
84. Carberry, Rev. John J., Ph.D., S.T.D., J.C.D., The Juridical Form of Marriage, X-177 pp., 1934.
85. Dolan, Rev. John L., A.B., J.C.D., The Defensor Vinculi, XII-157 pp., 1934.
86. Hannan, Rev. Jerome D., A.M., S.T.D., LL.B., J.C.D., The Canon Law of Wills, IX-517 pp., 1934.
87. Lemieux, Rev. Delise A., A.M., J.C.D., The Sentence in Ecclesiastical Procedure, IX-131 pp., 1934.
88. O'Rourke, Rev. James J., A.B., J.C.D., Parish Registers, VII-109 pp., 1934.
89. Timlin, Rev. Bartholomew, O.F.M., A.M., J.C.D., Conditional Matrimonial Consent, X-381 pp., 1934.

90. Wahl, Rev. Francis X., A.B., J.C.D., The Matrimonial Impediments of Consanguinity and Affinity, VI-125 pp., 1934.
91. White, Rev. Robert J., A.B., LL.B., S.T.B., J.C.D., Canonical Ante-Nuptial Promises and the Civil Law, VI-152 pp., 1934.
92. Herrera, Rev. Antonio Parra, O.C.D., J.C.D., Legislacion Ecclesiastica sobra el Ayuno y la Abstinencia, XI-191 pp., 1935.
93. Kennedy, Rev. Edwin J., J.C.D., The Special Matrimonial Process in Cases of Evident Nullity, X-165 pp., 1935.
94. Manning, Rev. John J., A.B., J.C.D., Presumption of Law in Matrimonial Procedure, XI-111 pp., 1935.
95. Moeder, Rev. John M., J.C.D., The Proper Bishop for Ordination and Dimissorial Letters, VII-135 pp., 1935.
96. O'Mara, Rev. William A., A.B., J.C.D., Canonical Causes for Matrimonial Dispensations, IX-155 pp., 1935.
97. Reilly, Rev. Peter, J.C.D., Residence of Pastors, IX-81 pp., 1935.
98. Smith, Rev. Mariner T., O.P., S.T.Lr., J.C.D., The Penal Law for Religious, VII-169 pp., 1935.
99. Whalen, Rev. Donald W., A.M., J.C.D., The Value of Testimonial Evidence in Matrimonial Procedure, XIII-297 pp., 1935.
100. Cleary, Rev. Joseph F., J.C.D., Canonical Limitations on the Alienation of Church Property, VIII-141 pp., 1936.
101. Glynn, Rev. John C., J.C.D., The Promoter of Justice, XX-337 pp., 1936.
102. Brennan, Rev. James H., S.S., M.A., S.T.B., J.C.D., The Simple Convalidation of Marriage, VI-135 pp., 1937.
103. Brunini, Rev. Joseph Bernard, J.C.D., The Clerical Obligations of Canons 139 and 142, X-121 pp., 1937.
104. Connor, Rev. Maurice, A.B., J.C.D., The Administrative Removal of Pastors, VIII-159 pp., 1937.
105. Guilfoyle, Rev. Merlin Joseph, J.C.D., Custom, XI-144 pp., 1937.
106. Hughes, Rev. James Austin, A.B., A.M., J.C.D., Witnesses in Criminal Trials of Clerics, IX-140 pp., 1937.
107. Jansen, Rev. Raymond J., A.B., S.T.L., J.C.D., Canonical Provisions for Catechetical Instruction, VII-153 pp., 1937.
108. Kealy, Rev. John James, A.B., J.C.D., The Introductory Libellus in Church Court Procedure, XI-121 pp., 1937.
109. McManus, Rev. James Edward, C.SS.R., J.C.D., The Administration of Temporal Goods in Religious Institutes, XVI-196 pp., 1937.
110. Moriarty, Rev. Eugene James, J.C.D., Oaths in Ecclesiastical Courts, X-115 pp., 1937.
111. Rainer, Rev. Eligius George, C.SS.R., J.C.D., Suspension of Clerics, XVII-249 pp., 1937.
112. Reilly, Rev. Thomas F., C.SS.R., J.C.D., Visitation of Religious, VI-195 pp., 1938.
113. Moriarity, Rev. Francis E., C.SS.R., J.C.D., The Extraordinary Absolution from Censures, XV-334 pp., 1938.

114. Connolly, Rev. Nicholas P., J.C.D., The Canonical Erection of Parishes, X-132 pp., 1938.
115. Donovan, Rev. James Joseph, J.C.D., The Pastor's Obligation in Prenuptial Investigation, XII-322 pp., 1938.
116. Harrigan, Rev. Robert J., M.A., S.T.B., J.C.D., The Radical Sanation of Invalid Marriages, VIII-208 pp., 1938.
117. Boffa, Rev. Conrad Humbert, J.C.D., Canonical Provisions for Catholic Schools, VII-211 pp., 1939.
118. Parsons, Rev. Anscar John, O.M.Cap., J.C.D., Canonical Elections, XII-236 pp., 1939.
119. Reilly, Rev. Edward Michael, A.B., J.C.D., The General Norms of Dispensation, XII-156 pp., 1939.
120. Ryan, Rev. Gerald Aloysius, A.B., J.C.D., Principles of Episcopal Jurisdiction, XII-172 pp., 1939.
121. Burton, Rev. Francis James, C.S.C., A.B., J.C.D., A Commentary on Canon 1125, XII-212 pp., 1940.
122. Miaskiewicz, Rev. Francis Sigismund, J.C.D., Supplied Jurisdiction According to Canon 209, XII-340 pp., 1940.
123. Rice, Rev. Patrick William, A.B., J.C.D., Proof of Death in Pre-Nuptial Investigation, VIII-156 pp., 1940.
124. Anglin, Rev. Thomas Francis, M.S., J.C.L., The Eucharistic Fast.
125. Coleman, Rev. John Jerome, J.C.L., The Minister of Confirmation.
126. Downs, Rev. John Emmanuel, A.B., J.C.L., The Concept of Clerical Immunity.
127. Esswein, Rev. Anthony Albert, J.C.L., Extrajudicial Penal Powers of Ecclesiastical Superiors.
128. Farrell, Rev. Benjamin Francis, M.A., S.T.L., J.C.L., The Rights and Duties of the Local Ordinary Regarding Congregations of Women Religious of Pontifical Approval.
129. Feeney, Rev. Thomas John, A.B., S.T.L., J.C.L., Restitutio in Integrum.
130. Findlay, Rev. Stephen Williams, O.S.B., A.B., J.C.L., Canonical Norms Governing the Deposition and Degradation of Clerics.
131. Goodwine, Rev. John, A.B., S.T.L., J.C.L., The Right of the Church to Acquire Property.
132. Heston, Rev. Edward Louis, C.S.C., Ph.D., S.T.D., J.C.L., The Alienation of Church Property in the United States.
133. Hogan, Rev. James John, S.T.L., J.C.L., Judicial Advocates and Procurators.
134. Kealy, Rev. Thomas M., A.B., LL.B., J.C.L., Dowry of Women Religious.
135. Keene, Rev. Michael James, O.S.B., J.C.L., Religious Ordinaries and Canon 198.
136. Kerin, Rev. Charles A., S.S., M.A., S.T.B., J.C.L., The Privation of Christian Burial.
137. Louis, Rev. William Francis, M.A., J.C.L., Diocesan Archives.

138. McDevitt, Rev. Gilbert Joseph, A.B., J.C.L., Legitimacy and Legitimation.
139. McDonough, Rev. Thomas Joseph, A.B., J.C.L., Apostolic Administrators.
140. Meier, Rev. Carl Anthony, A.B., J.C.L., Penal Administrative Procedure Against Negligent Pastors.
141. Schmidt, Rev. John Rogg, A.B., J.C.L., The Principles of Authentic Interpretation in Canon 17 of the Code of Canon Law.
142. Slafkosky, Rev. Andrew Leonard, A.B., J.C.L., The Canonical Episcopal Visitation of the Diocese.
143. Swoboda, Rev. Innocent Robert, O.F.M., J.C.L., Ignorance in Relation to the Impunity of Delicts.
144. Dube, Rev. Arthur Joseph, A.B., J.C.L., General Principles for the Reckoning of Time in Canon Law.
145. McBride, Rev. James T., A.B., J.C.L., Incardination and Excardination of Seculars.

www.ingramcontent.com/pod-product-compliance
Lightning Source LLC
LaVergne TN
LVHW050216080826
844660LV00012B/420

* 9 7 8 0 8 1 3 2 2 3 1 6 2 *